Charlotte M. Yonge

Young Folks' History Of Rome
Vol.I

Publisher : BoD · Books on Demand, 31 avenue Saint-Rémy,
57600 Forbach, bod@bod.fr
Print : Libri Plureos GmbH, Friedensallee 273,
22763 Hamburg (Allemagne)
ISBN : 978-2-3226-2251-1
Dépôt légal : Avril 2025

Young Folks' History Of Rome
Vol.I
By
Charlotte M. Yonge

YOUNG FOLKS' HISTORY OF ROME

CHAPTER I.
ITALY.

I am going to tell you next about the most famous nation in the world. Going westward from Greece another peninsula stretches down into the Mediterranean. The Apennine Mountains run like a limb stretching out of the Alps to the south eastward, and on them seems formed that land, shaped somewhat like a leg, which is called Italy.

Round the streams that flowed down from these hills, valleys of fertile soil formed themselves, and a great many different tribes and people took up their abode there, before there was any history to explain their coming. Putting together what can be proved about them, it is plain, however, that most of them came of that old stock from which the Greeks descended, and to which we belong ourselves, and they spoke a language which had the same root as ours and as the Greek. From one of these nations the best known form of this, as it was polished in later times, was called Latin, from the tribe who spoke it.

River Tiber
THE TIBER

About the middle of the peninsula there runs down, westward from the Apennines, a river called the Tiber, flowing rapidly between seven low hills, which recede as it approaches the sea. One, in especial, called the Palatine

Hill, rose separately, with a flat top and steep sides, about four hundred yards from the river, and girdled in by the other six. This was the place where the great Roman power grew up from beginnings, the truth of which cannot now be discovered.

Pottery
CURIOUS POTTERY.

There were several nations living round these hills—the Etruscans, Sabines, and Latins being the chief. The homes of these nations seem to have been in the valleys round the spurs of the Apennines, where they had farms and fed their flocks; but above them was always the hill which they had fortified as strongly as possible, and where they took refuge if their enemies attacked them. The Etruscans built very mighty walls, and also managed the drainage of their cities wonderfully well. Many of their works remain to this day, and, in especial, their monuments have been opened, and the tomb of each chief has been found, adorned with figures of himself, half lying, half sitting; also curious pottery in red and black, from which something of their lives and ways is to be made out. They spoke a different language from what has become Latin, and they had a different religion, believing in one great Soul of the World, and also thinking much of rewards and punishments after death. But we know hardly anything about them, except that their chiefs were called Lucumos, and that they once had a wide power which they had lost before the time of history. The Romans called them Tusci, and Tuscany still keeps its name.

The Latins and the Sabines were more alike, and also more like the Greeks. There were a great many settlements of Greeks in the southern parts of Italy, and they learnt something from them. They had a great many gods. Every house had its own guardian. These were called Lares, or Penates, and were generally represented as little figures of dogs lying by the hearth, or as brass bars with dogs' heads. This is the reason that the bars which close in an open hearth are still called dogs. Whenever there was a meal in the house the master began by pouring out wine to the Lares, and also to his own ancestors, of whom he kept figures; for these natives thought much of their families, and all one family had the same name, like our surname, such as Tullius or Appius, the daughters only changing it by making it end in a instead of us, and the men having separate names standing first, such as Marcus or Lucius, though their sisters were only numbered to distinguish them.

Jupiter
JUPITER

Each city had a guardian spirit, each stream its nymph, each wood its faun;

also there were gods to whom the boundary stones of estates were dedicated. There was a goddess of fruits called Pomona, and a god of fruits named Vertumnus. In their names the fields and the crops were solemnly blest, and all were sacred to Saturn. He, according to the old legends, had first taught husbandry, and when he reigned in Italy there was a golden age, when every one had his own field, lived by his own handiwork, and kept no slaves. There was a feast in honor of this time every year called the Saturnalia, when for a few days the slaves were all allowed to act as if they were free, and have all kinds of wild sports and merriment. Afterwards, when Greek learning came in, Saturn was mixed up with the Greek Kronos, or Time, who devours his offspring, and the reaping-hook his figures used to carry for harvest became Time's scythe. The sky-god, Zeus or Deus Pater (or father), was shortened into Jupiter; Juno was his wife, and Mars was god of war, and in Greek times was supposed to be the same as Ares; Pallas Athene was joined with the Latin Minerva; Hestia, the goddess of the hearth, was called Vesta; and, in truth, we talk of the Greek gods by their Latin names. The old Greek tales were not known to the Latins in their first times, but only afterwards learnt from the Greeks. They seem to have thought of their gods as graver, higher beings, further off, and less capricious and fanciful than the legends about the weather had made them seem to the Greeks. Indeed, these Latins were a harder, tougher, graver, fiercer, more business-like race altogether than the Greeks; not so clever, thoughtful, or poetical, but with more of what we should now call sterling stuff in them.

At least so it was with that great nation which spoke their language, and seems to have been an offshoot from them. Rome, the name of which is said to mean the famous, is thought to have been at first a cluster of little villages, with forts to protect them on the hills, and temples in the forts. Jupiter had a temple on the Capitoline Hill, with cells for his worship, and that of Juno and Minerva; and the two-faced Janus, the god of gates, had his upon the Janicular Hill. Besides these, there were the Palatine, the Esquiline, the Aventine, the Cælian, and the Quirinal. The people of these villages called themselves Quirites, or spearmen, when they formed themselves into an army and made war on their neighbors, the Sabines and Latins, and by-and-by built a wall enclosing all the seven hills, and with a strip of ground within, free from houses, where sacrifices were offered and omens sought for.

The history of these people was not written till long after they had grown to be a mighty and terrible power, and had also picked up many Greek notions. Then they seem to have made their history backwards, and worked up their old stories and songs to explain the names and customs they found among them, and the tales they told were formed into a great history by one Titus Livius. It is needful to know these stories which every one used to believe to be really history; so we will tell them first, beginning, however, with a story told by the poet Virgil.

CHAPTER II.
THE WANDERINGS OF ÆNEAS.

You remember in the Greek history the burning of Troy, and how Priam and all his family were cut off. Among the Trojans there was a prince called Æneas, whose father was Anchises, a cousin of Priam, and his mother was said to be the goddess Venus. When he saw that the city was lost, he rushed back to his house, and took his old father Anchises on his back, giving him his Penates, or little images of household gods, to take care of, and led by the hand his little son Iulus, or Ascanius, while his wife Creusa followed close behind, and all the Trojans who could get their arms together joined him, so that they escaped in a body to Mount Ida; but just as they were outside the city he missed poor Creusa, and though he rushed back and searched for her everywhere, he never could find her. For the sake of his care for his gods, and for his old father, he is always known as the pious Æneas.

In the forests of Mount Ida he built ships enough to set forth with all his followers in quest of the new home which his mother, the goddess Venus, gave him hopes of. He had adventures rather like those of Ulysses as he sailed about the Mediterranean. Once in the Strophades, some clusters belonging to the Ionian Islands, when he and his troops had landed to get food, and were eating the flesh of the numerous goats which they found climbing about the rocks, down on them came the harpies, horrible birds with women's faces and hooked hands, with which they snatched away the food and spoiled what they could not eat. The Trojans shot at them, but the arrows glanced off their feathers and did not hurt them. However, they all flew off except one, who sat on a high rock, and croaked out that the Trojans would be punished for thus molesting the harpies by being tossed about till they should reach Italy, but there they should not build their city till they should have been so hungry as to eat their very trenchers.

Coast
THE COAST.

They sailed away from this dismal prophetess, and touched on the coast of Epirus, where Æneas found his cousin Helenus, son to old Priam, reigning over a little new Troy, and married to Andromache, Hector's wife, whom he had gained after Pyrrhus had been killed. Helenus was a prophet, and gave Æneas much advice. In especial he said that when the Trojans should come to Italy, they would find, under the holly-trees by the river side, a large white old sow lying on the ground, with a litter of thirty little pigs round her, and this should be a sign to them where they were to build their city.

By his advice the Trojans coasted round the south of Sicily, instead of trying to pass the strait between the dreadful Scylla and Charybdis, and just below Mount Etna an unfortunate man came running down to the beach begging to be taken in. He was a Greek, who had been left behind when Ulysses escaped from Polyphemus' cave, and had made his way to the forests, where he had lived ever since. They had just taken him in when they saw Cyclops coming down, with a pine tree for a staff, to wash the burning hollow of his lost eye in the sea, and they rowed off in great terror.

Etna
MOUNT ETNA.

Poor old Anchises died shortly after, and while his son was still sorrowing for him, Juno, who hated every Trojan, stirred up a terrible tempest, which drove the ships to the south, until, just as the sea began to calm down, they came into a beautiful bay, enclosed by tall cliffs with woods overhanging them. Here the tired wanderers landed, and, lighting a fire, Æneas went in quest of food. Coming out of the forest, they looked down from a hill, and beheld a multitude of people building a city, raising walls, houses, towers, and temples. Into one of these temples Æneas entered, and to his amazement he found the walls sculptured with all the story of the siege of Troy, and all his friends so perfectly represented, that he burst into tears at the sight.

Just then a beautiful queen, attended by a whole troop of nymphs, came into the temple. This lady was Dido; her husband, Sichæus, had been king of Tyre, till he was murdered by his brother Pygmalion, who meant to have married her, but she fled from him with a band of faithful Tyrians and all her husband's treasure, and had landed on the north coast of Africa. There she begged of the chief of the country as much land as could be enclosed by a bullock's hide. He granted this readily; and Dido, cutting the hide into the finest possible strips, managed to measure off with it ground enough to build the splendid city which she had named Carthage. She received Æneas most kindly, and took all his men into her city, hoping to keep them there for ever, and make him her husband. Æneas himself was so happy there, that he forgot all his plans and the prophecies he had heard, until Jupiter sent Mercury to rouse him to fulfil his destiny. He obeyed the call; and Dido was so wretched at his departure that she caused a great funeral pile to be built, laid herself on the top, and stabbed herself with Æneas' sword; the pile was burnt, and the Trojans saw the flame from their ships without knowing the cause.

Carthage

CARTHAGE.

By-and-by Æneas landed at a place in Italy named Cumæ. There dwelt one of the Sybils. These were wondrous virgins whom Apollo had endowed with deep wisdom; and when Æneas went to consult the Cumæan Sybil, she told him that he must visit the under-world of Pluto to learn his fate. First, however, he had to go into a forest, and find there and gather a golden bough, which he was to bear in his hand to keep him safe. Long he sought it, until two doves, his mother's birds, came flying before him to show him the tree where gold gleamed through the boughs, and he found the branch growing on the tree as mistletoe grows on the thorn.

Guarded with this, and guided by the Sybil, after a great sacrifice, Æneas passed into a gloomy cave, where he came to the river Styx, round which flitted all the shades who had never received funeral rites, and whom the ferryman, Charon, would not carry over. The Sybil, however, made him take Æneas across, his boat groaning under the weight of a human body. On the other side stood Cerberus, but the Sybil threw him a cake of honey and of some opiate, and he lay asleep, while Æneas passed on and found in myrtle groves all who had died for love, among them, to his surprise, poor forsaken Dido. A little further on he found the home of the warriors, and held converse with his old Trojan friends. He passed by the place of doom for the wicked, Tartarus; and in the Elysian fields, full of laurel groves and meads of asphodel, he found the spirit of his father Anchises, and with him was allowed to see the souls of all their descendants, as yet unborn, who should raise the glory of their name. They are described on to the very time when the poet wrote to whom we owe all the tale of the wanderings of Æneas, namely, Virgil, who wrote the Æneid, whence all these stories are taken. He further tells us that Æneas landed in Italy just as his old nurse Caiëta died, at the place which is still called Gaëta. After they had buried her, they found a grove, where they sat down on the grass to eat, using large round cakes or biscuits to put their meat on. Presently they came to eating up the cakes. Little Ascanius cried out, "We are eating our very tables;" and Æneas, remembering the harpy's words, knew that his wanderings were over.

Soldier
ROMAN SOLDIER.

CHAPTER III.
THE FOUNDING OF ROME.

B.C. 753—713.

Virgil goes on to tell at much length how the king of the country, Latinus, at first made friends with Æneas, and promised him his daughter Lavinia in marriage; but Turnus, an Italian chief who had before been a suitor to Lavinia, stirred up a great war, and was only captured and killed after much hard fighting. However, the white sow was found in the right place with all her little pigs, and on the spot was founded the city of Alba Longa, where Æneas and Lavinia reigned until he died, and his descendants, through his two sons, Ascanius or Iulus, and Æneas Silvius, reigned after him for fifteen generations.

The last of these fifteen was Amulius, who took the throne from his brother Numitor, who had a daughter named Rhea Silvia, a Vestal virgin. In Greece, the sacred fire of the goddess Vesta was tended by good men, but in Italy it was the charge of maidens, who were treated with great honor, but were never allowed to marry under pain of death. So there was great anger when Rhea Silvia became the mother of twin boys, and, moreover, said that her husband was the god Mars. But Mars did not save her from being buried alive, while the two babes were put in a trough on the waters of the river Tiber, there to perish. The river had overflowed its banks, and left the children on dry ground, where, however, they were found by a she-wolf, who fondled and fed them like her own offspring, until a shepherd met with them and took them home to his wife. She called them Romulus and Remus, and bred them up as shepherds.

When the twin brothers were growing into manhood, there was a fight between the shepherds of Numitor and Amulius, in which Romulus and Remus did such brave feats that they were led before Numitor. He enquired into their birth, and their foster-father told the story of his finding them, showing the trough in which they had been laid; and thus it became plain that they were the grandsons of Numitor. On finding this out, they collected an army, with which they drove away Amulius, and brought their grandfather back to Alba Longa.

They then resolved to build a new city for themselves on one of the seven low hills beneath which ran the yellow river Tiber; but they were not agreed on which hill to build, Remus wanting to build on the Aventine Hill, and Romulus on the Palatine. Their grandfather advised them to watch for omens from the gods, so each stood on his hill and watched for birds. Remus was the first to see six vultures flying, but Romulus saw twelve, and therefore the Palatine Hill was made the beginning of the city, and Romulus was chosen king. Remus was affronted, and when the mud wall was being raised around the space intended for the city, he leapt over it and laughed, whereupon Romulus struck him dead, crying out, "So perish all who leap over the walls of my city."

Banquet
GLADIATORIAL SHOWS AT A BANQUET

Romulus traced out the form of the city with the plough, and made it almost a square. He called the name of it Rome, and lived in the midst of it in a mud-hovel, covered with thatch, in the midst of about fifty families of the old Trojan race, and a great many young men, outlaws and runaways from the neighboring states, who had joined him. The date of the building of Rome was supposed to be A.D. 753; and the Romans counted their years from it, as the Greeks did from the Olympiads, marking the date A.U.C., anno urbis conditæ, the year of the city being built. The youths who joined Romulus could not marry, as no one of the neighboring nations would give his daughter to one of these robbers, as they were esteemed. The nearest neighbors to Rome were the Sabines, and the Romans cast their eyes in vain on the Sabine ladies, till old Numitor advised Romulus to proclaim a great feast in honor of Neptune, with games and dances. All the people in the country round came to it, and when the revelry was at its height each of the unwedded Romans seized on a Sabine maiden and carried her away to his own house. Six hundred and eighty-three girls were thus seized, and the next day Romulus married them all after the fashion ever after observed in Rome. There was a great sacrifice, then each damsel was told, "Partake of your husband's fire and water;" he gave her a ring, and carried her over his threshold, where a sheepskin was spread, to show that her duty would be to spin wool for him, and she became his wife.

Forum
THE FORUM.

Romulus himself won his own wife, Hersilia, among the Sabines on this occasion; but the nation of course took up arms, under their king Tatius, to recover their daughters. Romulus drew out his troops into Campus Martius, or field of Mars, just beneath the Capitol, or great fort on the Saturnian Hill, and marched against the Sabines; but while he was absent, Tarpeia, the daughter of the governor of the little fort he had left on the Saturnian Hill, promised to let the Sabines in on condition they would give her what they wore on their left arms, meaning their bracelets; but they hated her treason even while they took advantage of it, and no sooner were they within the gate than they pelted her with their heavy shields, which they wore on their left arms, and killed her. The cliff on the top of which she died is still called the Tarpeian rock, and criminals were executed by being thrown from the top of it. Romulus tried to regain the Capitol, but the Sabines rolled down stones on the Romans, and he was stunned by one that struck him on the head; and though he quickly recovered and rallied his men, the battle was going against him, when all the Sabine women, who had been nearly two years Roman wives, came rushing out, with their little children in their arms and their hair flying, begging their fathers and husbands not to kill one another. This led to the making of a peace, and it was agreed that the Sabines and Romans should make but one nation, and that Romulus and Tatius should reign together at Rome. Romulus lived on the Palatine Hill, Tatius on the Tarpeian, and the valley between was called the Forum, and was the market-place, and also the spot where all public assemblies were held. All the chief arrangements for war and government were believed by the Romans to have been laws of Romulus. However, after five years, Tatius was murdered at a place called Lavinium, in the middle of a sacrifice, and Romulus reigned alone till in the middle of a great assembly of his soldiers outside the city, a storm of thunder and lightning came on, and every one hurried home, but the king was nowhere to be found; for, as some say, his father Mars had come down in the tempest and carried him away to reign with the gods, while others declared that he was murdered by persons, each of whom carried home a fragment of his body that it might never be found. It matters less which way we tell it, since the story of Romulus was quite as much a fable as that of Æneas; only it must be remembered as the Romans themselves believed it. They worshipped Romulus under the name of Quirinus, and called their chief families Quirites, both words coming from ger (a spear); and the she-wolf and twins were the favorite badge of the empire. The Capitoline Hill, the Palatine, and the Forum all still bear the same names.

tration

CHAPTER IV.
NUMA AND TULLUS.

B.C. 713—618.

It was understood between the Romans and the Sabines that they should have by turns a king from each nation, and, on the disappearance of Romulus, a Sabine was chosen, named Numa Pompilius, who had been married to Tatia, the daughter of the Sabine king Tatius, but she was dead, and had left one daughter. Numa had, ever since her death, been going about from one grove or fountain sacred to the gods to another offering up sacrifices, and he was much beloved for his gentleness and wisdom. There was a grove near Rome, in a valley, where a fountain gushed forth from the rock; and here Egeria, the nymph of the stream, in the shade of the trees, counselled Numa on his government, which was so wise that he lived at peace with all his neighbors. When the Romans doubted whether it was really a goddess who inspired him, Egeria convinced them, for the next time he had any guests in his house, the earthenware plates with homely fare on them were changed before their eyes into golden dishes with dainty food. Moreover, there was brought from heaven a bronze shield, which was to be carefully kept, since Rome would never fall while it was safe. Numa had eleven other shields like it made and hung in the temple of Mars, and, yearly, a set of men dedicated to the office bore them through the city with songs and dances. Just as all warlike customs were said to have been invented by Romulus, all peaceful and religious ones were held to have sprung from Numa and his Egeria. He was said to have fixed the calendar and invented the names of the months, and to have built an altar to Good Faith to teach the Romans to keep their word to one another and to all nations, and to have dedicated the bounds of each estate to the Dii Termini, or Landmark Gods, in whose honor there was a feast yearly. He also was said to have had such power with Jupiter as to have persuaded him to be content without receiving sacrifices of men and women. In short, all the better things in the Roman system were supposed to be due to the gentle Numa.

At the gate called Janiculum stood a temple to the watchman god Janus, whose figure had two faces, and held the keys, and after whom was named the month January. His temple was always open in time of war, and closed in time of peace. Numa's reign was counted as the first out of only three times in Roman history that it was shut.

Janus
JANUS.

Numa was said to have reigned thirty-eight years, and then he gradually faded away, and was buried in a stone coffin outside the Janicular gate, all the books he had written being, by his desire, buried with him. Egeria wept till she became a fountain in her own valley; and so ended what in Roman faith answered to the golden age of Greece.

The next king was of Roman birth, and was named Tullus Hostilius. He was a great warrior, and had a war with the Albans until it was agreed that the two cities should join together in one, as the Romans and Sabines had done before; but there was a dispute which should be the greater city in the league and it was determined to settle it by a combat. In each city there was a family where three sons had been born at a birth, and their mothers were sisters. Both sets were of the same age—fine young men, skilled in weapons; and it was agreed that the six should fight together, the three whose family name was Horatius on the Roman side, the three called Curiatius on the Alban side, and whichever set gained the mastery was to give it to his city.

They fought in the plain between the camps, and very hard was the strife until two of the Horatii were killed and all the three Curiatii were wounded, but the last Horatius was entirely untouched. He began to run, and his cousins pursued him, but at different distances, as one was less hindered by his wound than the others. As soon as the first came up. Horatius slew him, and so the second and the third: as he cut down this last he cried out, "To the glory of Rome I sacrifice thee." As the Alban king saw his champion fall, he turned to Tullus Hostilius and asked what his commands were. "Only to have the Alban youth ready when I need them," said Tullus.

A wreath was set on the victor's head, and, loaded with the spoil of the Curiatii, he was led into the city in triumph. His sister came hurrying to meet him; she was betrothed to one of the Curiatii, and was in agony to know his fate; and when she saw the garment she had spun for him hanging blood-stained over her brother's shoulders, she burst into loud lamentations. Horatius, still hot with fury, struck her dead on the spot, crying, "So perish every Roman who mourns the death of an enemy of his country." Even her father approved the cruel deed, and would not bury her in his family tomb—so stern were Roman feelings, putting the honor of the country above everything. However, Horatius was brought before the king for the murder, and was sentenced to die; but the people entreated that their champion might be spared, and he was only made to pass under what was called the yoke, namely, spears set up like a doorway.

Tullus Hostilius gained several victories over his neighbors, but he was harsh and presuming, and offended the gods, and, when he was using some spell such as good Numa had used to hold converse with Jupiter, the angry god sent lightning and burnt up him and his family. The people then chose Ancus Martins, the son of Numa's daughter, who is said to have ruled in his grandfather's spirit, though he could not avoid wars with the Latins. The first bridge over the Tiber, named the Sublician, was said to have been built by him. In his time there came to Rome a family called Tarquin. Their father was a Corinthian, who had settled in an Etruscan town named Tarquinii, whence came the family name. He was said to have first taught writing in Italy, and, indeed, the Roman letters which we still use are Greek letters made simpler. His eldest son, finding that because of his foreign blood he could rise to no honors in Etruria, set off with his wife Tanaquil, and their little son Lucius Tarquinius, to settle in Rome. Just as they came in sight of Rome, an eagle swooped down from the sky, snatched off little Tarquin's cap, and flew up with it, but the next moment came down again and put it back on his head. On this Tanaquil foretold that her son would be a great king, and he became so famous a warrior when he grew up, that, as the children of Ancus were too young to reign at their father's death, he was chosen king. He is said to have been the first Roman king who wore a purple robe and golden crown, and in the valley between the Palatine and Aventine Hills he made a circus, where games could be held like those of the Greeks; also he placed stone benches and stalls for shops round the Forum, and built a stone wall instead of a mud one round the city. He is commonly called Tarquinus Priscus, or the elder.

Actors
ACTORS

There was a fair slave girl in his house, who was offering cakes to Lar, the household spirit, when he appeared to her in bodily form. When she told the king's mother, Tanaquil, she said it was a token that he wanted to marry her, and arrayed her as a bride for him. Of this marriage there sprang a boy called Servius Tullus. When this child lay asleep, bright flames played about his head, and Tanaquil knew he would be great, so she caused her son Tarquin to give him his daughter in marriage when he grew up. This greatly offended the two sons of Ancus Martius, and they hired two young men to come before him as wood-cutters, with axes over their shoulders, pretending to have a quarrel about some goats, and while he was listening to their cause they cut him down and mortally wounded him. He had lost his sons, and had only two baby grandsons, Aruns and Tarquin, who could not reign as yet; but while he was dying, Tanaquil stood at the window and declared that he was only stunned and would soon be well. This, as she intended, so frightened the sons of Ancus that they fled from Rome; and Servius Tullus, coming forth in the royal robes, was at once hailed as king by all the people of Rome, being thus made king that he might protect his wife's two young nephews, the two little Tarquins.

CHAPTER V.
THE DRIVING OUT OF THE TARQUINS.

B.C. 578—309.

Servius Tullus was looked on by the Romans as having begun making their laws, as Romulus had put their warlike affairs in order, and Numa had settled their religion. The Romans were all in great clans or families, all with one name, and these were classed in tribes. The nobler ones, who could count up from old Trojan, Latin, or Sabine families, were called Patricians—from pater, a father—because they were fathers of the people; and the other families were called Plebeian, from plebs, the people. The patricians formed the Senate or Council of Government, and rode on horseback in war, while the plebeians fought on foot. They had spears, round shields, and short pointed swords, which cut on each side of the blade. Tullus is said to have fixed how many men of each tribe should be called out to war. He also walled in the city again with a wall five miles round; and he made many fixed laws, one being that when a man was in debt his goods might be seized, but he himself might not be made a slave. He was the great friend of the plebeians, and first established the rule that a new law of the Senate could not be made without the consent of the Comitia, or whole free people.

The Sabines and Romans were still striving for the mastery, and a husbandman among the Sabines had a wonderfully beautiful cow. An oracle declared that the man who sacrificed this cow to Diana upon the Aventine Hill would secure the chief power to his nation. The Sabine drove the cow to Rome, and was going to kill her, when a crafty Roman priest told him that he must first wash his hands in the Tiber, and while he was gone sacrificed the cow himself, and by this trick secured the rule to Rome. The great horns of the cow were long after shown in the temple of Diana on the Aventine, where Romans, Sabines, and Latins every year joined in a great sacrifice.

The two daughters of Servius were married to their cousins, the two young Tarquins. In each pair there was a fierce and a gentle one. The fierce Tullia was the wife of the gentle Aruns Tarquin; the gentle Tulla had married the proud Lucius Tarquin. Aruns' wife tried to persuade her husband to seize the throne that had belonged to his father, and when he would not listen to her, she agreed with his brother Lucius that, while he murdered her sister, she should kill his brother, and then that they should marry. The horrid deed was carried out, and old Servius, seeing what a wicked pair were likely to come after him, began to consider with the Senate whether it would not be better to have two consuls or magistrates chosen every year than a king. This made Lucius Tarquin the more furious, and going to the Senate, where the patricians hated the king as the friend of the plebeians, he stood upon the throne, and was beginning to tell the patricians that this would be the ruin of their greatness, when Servius came in and, standing on the steps of the doorway, ordered him to come down. Tarquin sprang on the old man and hurled him backward, so that the fall killed him, and his body was left in the street. The wicked Tullia, wanting to know how her husband had sped, came out in her chariot on that road. The horses gave back before the corpse. She asked what was in their way; the slave who drove her told her it was the king's body. "Drive on," she said. The horrid deed caused the street to be known ever after as "Sceleratus," or the wicked. But it was the plebeians who mourned for Servius; the patricians in their anger made Tarquin king, but found him a very hard and cruel master, so that he is generally called Tarquinius Superbus, or Tarquin the proud. In his time the Sybil of Cumæ, the same wondrous maiden of deep wisdom who had guided Æneas to the realms of Pluto, came, bringing nine books of prophecies of the history of Rome, and offered them to him at a price which he thought too high, and refused. She went away, destroyed three, and brought back the other six, asking for them double the price of the whole. He refused. She burnt three more, and brought him the last three with the price again doubled, because the fewer they were, the more precious. He bought them at last, and placed them in the Capitol, whence they were now and then taken to be consulted as oracles.

Cave
SYBIL'S CAVE.

Rome was at war with the city of Gabii, and as the city was not to be subdued by force, Tarquin tried treachery. His eldest son, Sextus Tarquinius, fled to Gabii, complaining of ill-usage of his father, and showing marks of a severe scourging. The Gabians believed him, and he was soon so much trusted by them as to have the whole command of the army and manage everything in the city. Then he sent a messenger to his father to ask what he was to do next. Tarquin was walking through a cornfield. He made no answer in words, but with a switch cut off the heads of all the poppies and taller stalks of corn, and bade the messenger tell Sextus what he had seen. Sextus understood, and contrived to get all the chief men of Gabii exiled or put to death, and without them the city fell an easy prey to the Romans.

Tarquin sent his two younger sons and their cousin to consult the oracle at Delphi, and with them went Lucius Junius, who was called Brutus because he was supposed to be foolish, that being the meaning of the word; but his folly was only put on, because he feared the jealousy of his cousins. After doing their father's errand, the two Tarquins asked who should rule Rome after their father. "He," said the priestess, "who shall first kiss his mother on his return." The two brothers agreed that they would keep this a secret from their elder brother Sextus, and, as soon as they reached home, both of them rushed into the women's rooms, racing each to be the first to embrace their mother Tullia; but at the very entrance of Rome Brutus pretended to slip, threw himself on the ground and kissed his Mother Earth, having thus guessed the right meaning of the answer.

He waited patiently, however, and still was thought a fool when the army went out to besiege the city of Ardea; and while the troops were encamped round it, some of the young patricians began to dispute which had the best wife. They agreed to put it to the test by galloping late in the evening to look in at their homes and see what their wives were about. Some were idling, some were visiting, some were scolding, some were dressing, some were asleep; but at Collatia, the farm of another of the Tarquin family, thence called Collatinus, they found his beautiful wife Lucretia among her maidens spinning the wool of the flocks. All agreed that she was the best of wives; but the wicked Sextus Tarquin only wanted to steal her from her husband, and going by night to Collatia, tried to make her desert her lord, and when she would not listen to him he ill-treated her cruelly, and told her that he should accuse her to her husband. She was so overwhelmed with grief and shame that in the morning she sent for her father and husband, told them all that that happened, and saying that she could not bear life after being so put to shame, she drew out a dagger and stabbed herself before their eyes—thinking, as all these heathen Romans did, that it was better to die by one's own hand than to live in disgrace.

Lucius Brutus had gone to Collatia with his cousin, and while Collatinus and his father-in-law stood horror-struck, he called to them to revenge this crime. Snatching the dagger from Lucretia's breast, he galloped to Rome, called the people together in the Forum, and, holding up the bloody weapon in his hand, he made them a speech, asking whether they would any longer endure such a family of tyrants. They all rose as one man, and choosing Brutus himself and Collatinus to be their leaders, as the consuls whom Servius Tullus had thought of making, they shut the gates of Rome, and would not open them when Tarquin and his sons would have returned. So ended the kingdom of Rome.

tration

CHAPTER VI.
THE WAR WITH PORSENA.

From the time of the flight of the Tarquins, Rome was governed by two consuls, who wore all the tokens of royalty except the crown. Tarquin fled into Etruria, whence his grandfather had come, and thence tried to obtain admission into Rome. The two young sons of Brutus and the nephews of Collatinus were drawn into a plot for bringing them back again, and on its discovery were brought before the two consuls. Their guilt was proved, and their father sternly asked what they had to say in their defence. They only wept, and so did Collatinus and many of the senators, crying out, "Banish them, banish them." Brutus, however, as if unmoved, bade the executioners do their office. The whole Senate shrieked to hear a father thus condemn his own children, but he was resolute, and actually looked on while the young men were first scourged and then beheaded.

Collatinus put off the further judgment in hopes to save his nephews, and Brutus told them that he had put them to death by his own power as a father, but that he left the rest to the voice of the people, and they were sent into banishment. Even Collatinus was thought to have acted weakly, and was sent into exile—so determined were the Romans to have no one among them who would not uphold their decrees to the utmost. Tarquin advanced to the walls and cut down all the growing corn around the Campus Martius and threw it into the Tiber; there it formed a heap round which an island was afterwards formed. Brutus himself and his cousin Aruns Tarquin soon after killed one another in single combat in a battle outside the walls, and all the women of Rome mourned for him as for a father.

Tarquin found a friend in the Etruscan king called Lars Porsena, who brought an army to besiege Rome and restore him to the throne. He advanced towards the gate called Janiculum upon the Tiber, and drove the Romans out of the fort on the other side the river. The Romans then retreated across the bridge, placing three men to guard it until all should be gone over and it could be broken down.

Brutus
BRUTUS CONDEMNING HIS SONS.

There stood the brave three—Horatius, Lartius, and Herminius—guarding the bridge while their fellow-citizens were fleeing across it, three men against a whole army. At last the weapons of Lartius and Herminius were broken down, and Horatius bade them hasten over the bridge while it could still bear their weight. He himself fought on till he was wounded in the thigh, and the last timbers of the bridge were falling into the stream. Then spreading out his arms, he called upon Father Tiber to receive him, leapt into the river and swam across amid a shower of arrows, one of which put out his eye, and he was lame for life. A statue of him "halting on his thigh" was set up in the temple of Vulcan, and he was rewarded with as much land as one yoke of oxen could plough in a day, and the 300,000 citizens of Rome each gave him a day's provision of corn.

Porsena then blockaded the city, and when the Romans were nearly starving he sent them word that he would give them food if they would receive their old masters; but they made answer that hunger was better than slavery, and still held out. In the midst of their distress, a young man named Caius Mucius came and begged leave of the consuls to cross the Tiber and go to attempt something to deliver his country. They gave leave, and creeping through the Etruscan camp he came into the king's tent just as Porsena was watching his troops pass by in full order. One of his counsellors was sitting beside him so richly dressed that Mucius did not know which was king, and leaping towards them, he stabbed the counsellor to the heart. He was seized at once and dragged before the king, who fiercely asked who he was, and what he meant by such a crime.

The young man answered that his name was Caius Mucius, and that he was ready to do and dare anything for Rome. In answer to threats of torture, he quietly stretched out his right hand and thrust it into the flame that burnt in a brazier close by, holding it there without a sign of pain, while he bade Porsena see what a Roman thought of suffering.

Porsena was so struck that he at once gave the daring man his life, his freedom, and even his dagger; and Mucius then told him that three hundred youths like himself had sworn to have his life unless he left Rome to her liberty. This was false, but both the lie and the murder were for Rome's sake; they were both admired by the Romans, who held that the welfare of their city was their very first duty. Mucius could never use his right hand again, and was always called Scævola, or the Left-handed, a name that went on to his family.

Porsena believed the story, and began to make peace. A truce was agreed on, and ten Roman youths and as many girls were given up to the Etruscans as hostages. While the conferences were going on, one of the Roman girls named Clelia forgot her duty so much as to swim home across the river with all her companions; but Valeria, the consul's daughter, was received with all the anger that breach of trust deserved, and her father mounted his horse at once to take the party back again. Just as they reached the Etruscan camp, the Tarquin father and brothers, and a whole troop of the enemy, fell on them. While the consul was fighting against a terrible force, Valeria dashed on into the camp and called out Porsena and his son. They, much grieved that the truce should have been broken, drove back their own men, and were so angry with the Tarquins as to give up their cause. He asked which of the girls had contrived the escape, and when Clelia confessed it was herself, he made her a present of a fine horse and its trappings, which she little deserved.

This Valerius was called Publicola, or the people's friend. He died a year or two later, after so many victories that the Romans honored him among their greatest heroes. Tarquin still continued to seek support among the different Italian nations, and again attacked the Romans with the help of the Latins. The chief battle was fought close to Lake Reg; Aulus Posthumius was the commander, but Marcus Valerius, brother to Publicola, was general of the horse. He had vowed to build a temple to Castor and Pollux if the Romans gained the victory; and in the beginning of the fight, two glorious youths of god-like stature appeared on horseback at the head of the Roman horse and fought for them. It was a very hard-fought battle. Valerius was killed, but so was Titus Tarquin, and the Latin force was entirely broken and routed. That same evening the two youths rode into the Forum, their horses dripping with sweat and their weapons bloody. They drew up and washed themselves at a fountain near the temple of Vesta, and as the people crowded round they told of the great victory, and while one man named Domitius doubted of it, since the Lake Reg was too far off for tidings to have come so fast, one of them laid his hand on the doubter's beard and changed it in a moment from black to copper color, so that he came to be called Domitius Ahenobarbus, or Brazen-beard. Then they disappeared, and the next morning Posthumius' messenger brought the news. The Romans had no doubt that these were indeed the glorious twins, and built their temple, as Valerius had vowed.

Ensigns
ROMAN ENSIGNS, STANDARDS, TRUMPETS ETC.

Tarquin had lost all his sons, and died in wretched exile at Cumæ. And here ends what is looked on as the legendary history of Rome, for though most of these stories have dates, and some sound possible, there is so much that is plainly untrue mixed up with them, that they can only be looked on as the old stories which were handed down to account for the Roman customs and copied by their historians.

tration

CHAPTER VII.
THE ROMAN GOVERNMENT.

So far as true history can guess, the Romans really did have kings and drove them out, but there are signs that, though Porsena was a real king, the war was not so honorable to the Romans as they said, for he took the city and made them give up all their weapons to him, leaving them nothing but their tools for husbandry. But they liked to forget their misfortunes.

The older Roman families were called patricians, or fathers, and thought all rights to govern belonged to them. Settlers who came in later were called plebeians, or the people, and at first had no rights at all, for all the land belonged to the patricians, and the only way for the plebeians to get anything done for them was to become hangers-on—or, as they called it, clients—of some patrician who took care of their interests. There was a council of patricians called the Senate, chosen among themselves, and also containing by right all who had been chief magistrates. The whole assembly of the patricians was called the Comitia. They, as has been said before, fought on horseback, while the plebeians fought on foot; but out of the rich plebeians a body was formed called the knights, who also used horses, and wore gold rings like the patricians.

Jupiter
HEAD OF JUPITER.

But the plebeians were always trying not to be left out of everything. By and by, they said under Servius Tullius, the city was divided into six quarters, and all the families living in them into six tribes, each of which had a tribune to watch over it, bring up the number of its men, and lead them to battle. Another division of the citizens, both patrician and plebeian, was made every five years. They were all counted and numbered and divided off into centuries according to their wealth. Then these centuries, or hundreds, had votes, by the persons they chose, when it was a question of peace or war. Their meeting was called the Comitia; but as there were more patrician centuries than plebeian ones, the patricians still had much more power. Besides, the Senate and all the magistrates were in those days always patricians. These magistrates were chosen every year. There were two consuls, who were like kings for the time, only that they wore no crowns; they had purple robes, and sat in chairs ornamented with ivory, and they were always attended by lictors, who carried bundles of rods tied round an axe—the first for scourging, the second for beheading. There were under them two prætors, or judges, who tried offences; two quæstors, who attended to the public buildings; and two censors, who had to look after the numbering and registering of the people in their tribes and centuries. The consuls in general commanded the army, but sometimes, when there was a great need, one single leader was chosen and was called dictator. Sometimes a dictator was chosen merely to fulfil an omen, by driving a nail into the head of the great statue of Jupiter in the Capitol. Besides these, all the priests had to be patricians; the chief of all was called Pontifex Maximus. Some say this was because he was the fax (maker) of pontes (bridges), as he blessed them and decided by omens where they should be; but others think the word was Pompifex, and that he was the maker of pomps or ceremonies. There were many priests as well as augurs, who had to draw omens from the flight of birds or the appearance of sacrifices, and who kept the account of the calendar of lucky and unlucky days, and of festivals.

Costumes
FEMALE COSTUMES.

The Romans were a grave religious people in those days, and did not count their lives or their affections dear in comparison with their duties to their altars and their hearths, though their notions of duty do not always agree with ours. Their dress in the city was a white woollen garment edged with purple—it must have been more like in shape to a Scottish plaid than anything else—and was wrapped round so as to leave one arm free: sometimes a fold was drawn over the head. No one might wear it but a free-born Roman, and he never went out on public business without it, even when more convenient fashions had been copied from Greece. Those who were asking votes for a public office wore it white (candidus), and therefore were called candidates. The consuls had it on great days entirely purple and embroidered, and all senators and ex-magistrates had broader borders of purple. The ladies wore a long graceful wrapping-gown; the boys a short tunic, and round their necks was hung a hollow golden ball called a bulla, or bubble. When a boy was seventeen, there was a great family sacrifice to the Lares and the forefathers, his bulla was taken off, the toga was put on, and he was enrolled by his own prænomen, Caius or Lucius, or whatever it might be, for there was only a choice of fifteen. After this he was liable to be called out to fight. A certain number of men were chosen from each tribe by the tribune. It was divided into centuries, each led by a centurion; and the whole body together was called a legion, from lego, to choose. In later times the proper number for a legion was 6000 men. Each legion had a standard, a bar across the top of the spear, with the letters on it S P Q R—Senatus, Populus Que Romanus—meaning the Roman Senate and People, a purple flag below and a figure above, such as an eagle, or the wolf and twins, or some emblem dear to the Romans. The legions were on foot, but the troops of patricians and knights on horseback were attached to them and had to protect them.

Costumes
FEMALE COSTUMES.

The Romans had in those days very small riches, they held in general small farms in the country, which they worked themselves with the help of their sons and slaves. The plebeians were often the richest. They too held farms leased to them by the state, and had often small shops in Rome. The whole territory was so small that it was easy to come into Rome to worship, attend the Senate, or vote, and many had no houses in the city. Each man was married with a ring and sacrifice, and the lady was then carried over the threshold, on which a sheepskin was spread, and made mistress of the house by being bidden to be Caia to Caius. The Roman matrons were good and noble women in those days, and the highest praise of them was held to be Domum mansit, lanam fecit— she stayed at home and spun wool. Each man was absolute master in his own house, and had full power over his grown-up sons, even for life or death, and they almost always submitted entirely. For what made the Romans so great was that they were not only brave, but they were perfectly obedient, and obeyed as perfectly as they could their fathers, their officers, their magistrates, and, as they thought, their gods.

CHAPTER VIII.
MENENIUS AGRIPPA'S FABLE.

B.C. 494.

A great deal of the history of Rome consists of struggles between the patricians and plebeians. In those early days the plebeians were often poor, and when they wanted to improve their lands they had to borrow money from the patricians, who not only had larger lands, but, as they were the officers in war, got a larger share of the spoil. The Roman law was hard on a man in debt. His lands might be seized, he might be thrown into prison or sold into slavery with his wife and children, or, if the creditors liked, be cut to pieces so that each might take his share.

One of these debtors, a man who was famous for bravery as a centurion, broke out of his prison and ran into the Forum, all in rags and with chains still hanging to his hands and feet, showing them to his fellow-citizens, and asking if this was just usage of a man who had done no crime. They were very angry, and the more because one of the consuls, Appius Claudius, was known to be very harsh, proud and cruel, as indeed were all his family. The Volscians, a tribe often at war with them, broke into their land at the same time, and the Romans were called to arms, but the plebeians refused to march until their wrongs were redressed. On this the other consul, Servilius, promised that a law should be made against keeping citizens in prison for debt or making slaves of their children; and thereupon the army assembled, marched against the enemy, and defeated them, giving up all the spoil to his troops. But the senate, when the danger was over, would not keep its promises, and even appointed a Dictator to put the plebeians down. Thereupon they assembled outside the walls in a strong force, and were going to attack the patricians, when the wise old Menenius Agrippa was sent out to try to pacify them. He told them a fable, namely, that once upon a time all the limbs of a man's body became disgusted with the service they had to render to the belly. The feet and legs carried it about, the hands worked for it and carried food to it, the mouth ate for it, and so on. They thought it hard thus all to toil for it, and agreed to do nothing for it—neither to carry it about, clothe it, nor feed it. But soon all found themselves growing weak and starved, and were obliged to own that all would perish together unless they went on waiting on this seemingly useless belly. So Agrippa told them that all ranks and states depended on one another, and unless all worked together all must be confusion and go to decay. The fable seems to have convinced both rich and poor; the debtors were set free and the debts forgiven. And though the laws about debts do not seem to have been changed, another law was made which gave the plebeians tribunes in peace as well as war. These tribunes were always to be plebeians, chosen by their own fellows. No one was allowed to hurt them during their year of office, on pain of being declared accursed and losing his property; and they had the power of stopping any decision of the senate by saying solemnly, Veto, I forbid. They were called tribunes of the people, while the officers in war were called military tribunes; and as it was on the Mons Sacer, or Sacred Mount, that this was settled, these laws were called the Leges Sacrariæ. An altar to the Thundering Jupiter was built to consecrate them: and, in gratitude for his management, Menenius Agrippa was highly honored all his life, and at his death had a public funeral.

But the struggles of the plebeians against the patricians were not by any means over. The Roman land—Agri (acre), it was called—had at first been divided in equal shares—at least so it was said—but as belonging to the state all the time, and only held by the occupier. As time went on, some persons of course gathered more into their own hands, and others of spendthrift or unfortunate families became destitute. Then there was an outcry that, as the lands belonged to the whole state, it ought to take them all back and divide them again more equally: but the patricians naturally regarded themselves as the owners, and would not hear of this scheme, which we shall hear of again and again by the name of the Agrarian Law. One of the patricians, who had thrice been consul, by name Spurius Cassius, did all he could to bring it about, but though the law was passed he could not succeed in getting it carried out. The patricians hated him, and a report got abroad that he was only gaining favor with the people in order to get himself made king. This made even the plebeians turn against him as a traitor; he was condemned by the whole assembly of the people, and beheaded, after being scourged by the lictors. The people soon mourned for their friend, and felt that they had been deceived in giving him up to their enemies. The senate would not execute his law, and the plebeians would not enlist in the next war, though the senate threatened to cut down the fruit trees and destroy the crops of every man who refused to join the army. When they were absolutely driven into the ranks, they even refused to draw their swords in face of the enemy, and would not gain a victory lest their consul should have the honor of it.

Palace
SENATORIAL PALACE.

This consul's name was Kæso Fabius. He belonged to a very clever, wary family, whose name it was said was originally Foveus (ditch), because they had first devised a plan of snaring wolves in pits or ditches. They were thought such excellent defenders of the claims of the patricians that for seven years following one or other of the Fabii was chosen consul. But by-and-by they began either to see that the plebeians had rights, or that they should do best by siding with them, for they went over to them; and when Kæso next was consul he did all he could to get the laws of Cassius carried out, but the senate were furious with him, and he found it was not safe to stay in Rome when his consulate was over. So he resolved at any rate to do good to his country. The Etruscans often came over the border and ravaged the country; but there was a watch-tower on the banks of the little river Cremera, which flows into the Tiber, and Fabius offered, with all the men of his name—306 in number, and 4000 clients—to keep guard there against the enemy. For some time they prospered there, and gained much spoil from the Etruscans; but at last the whole Etruscan army came against them, showing only a small number at first to tempt them out to fight, then falling on them with the whole force and killing the whole of them, so that of the whole name there remained only one boy of fourteen who had been left behind at Rome. And what was worse, the consul, Titus Menenius, was so near the army that he could have saved the Fabii, but for the hatred the patricians bore them as deserters from their cause.

Harbor
VIEW OF A ROMAN HARBOR.

However, the tribune Publilius gained for the plebeians that there should be five tribunes instead of two, and made a change in the manner of electing them which prevented the patricians from interfering. Also it was decreed that to interrupt a tribune in a public speech deserved death. But whenever an Appius Claudius was consul he took his revenge, and was cruelly severe, especially in the camp, where the consul as general had much more power than in Rome. Again the angry plebeians would not fight, but threw down their arms in sight of the enemy. Claudius scourged and beheaded; they endured grimly and silently, knowing that when he returned to Rome and his consulate was over their tribunes would call him to account. And so they did, and before all the tribes of Rome summoned him to answer for his savage treatment of free Roman citizens. He made a violent answer, but he saw how it would go with him, and put himself to death to avoid the sentence. So were the Romans proving again and again the truth of Agrippa's parable, that nothing can go well with body or members unless each will be ready to serve the other.

CHAPTER IX.
CORIOLANUS AND CINCINNATUS.

B.C. 458.

All the time these struggles were going on between the patricians and the plebeians at home, there were wars with the neighboring tribes, the Volscians, the Veians, the Latins, and the Etruscans. Every spring the fighting men went out, attacked their neighbors, drove off their cattle, and tried to take some town; then fought a battle, and went home to reap the harvest, gather the grapes and olives in the autumn, and attend to public business and vote for the magistrates in the winter. They were small wars, but famous men fought in them. In a war against the Volscians, when Cominius was consul, he was besieging a city called Corioli, when news came that the men of Antium were marching against him, and in their first attack on the walls the Romans were beaten off, but a gallant young patrician, descended from the king Ancus Marcius, Caius Marcius by name, rallied them and led them back with such spirit that the place was taken before the hostile army came up; then he fought among the foremost and gained the victory. When he was brought to the consul's tent covered with wounds, Cominius did all he could to show his gratitude—set on the young man's head the crown of victory, gave him the surname of Coriolanus in honor of his exploits, and granted him the tenth part of the spoil of ten prisoners. Of them, however, Coriolanus only accepted one, an old friend of the family, whom he set at liberty at once. Afterwards, when there was a great famine in Rome, Coriolanus led an expedition to Antium, and brought away quantities of corn and cattle, which he distributed freely, keeping none for himself.

But though he was so free of hand, Coriolanus was a proud, shy man, who would not make friends with the plebeians, and whom the tribunes hated as much as he despised them. He was elected consul, and the tribunes refused to permit him to become one; and when a shipload of wheat arrived from Sicily, there was a fierce quarrel as to how it should be distributed. The tribunes impeached him before the people for withholding it from them, and by the vote of a large number of citizens he was banished from Roman lands. His anger was great, but quiet. He went without a word away from the Forum to his house, where he took leave of his mother Veturia, his wife Volumnia, and his little children, and then went and placed himself by the hearth of Tullus the Volscian chief, in whose army he meant to fight to revenge himself upon his countrymen.

Together they advanced upon the Roman territory, and after ravaging the country threatened to besiege Rome. Men of rank came out and entreated him to give up this wicked and cruel vengeance, and to have pity on his friends and native city; but he answered that the Volscians were now his nation, and nothing would move him. At last, however, all the women of Rome came forth, headed by his mother Veturia and his wife Volumnia, each with a little child, and Veturia entreated and commanded her son in the most touching manner to change his purpose and cease to ruin his country, begging him, if he meant to destroy Rome, to begin by slaying her. She threw herself at his feet as she spoke, and his hard spirit gave way.

"Ah! mother, what is it you do?" he cried as he lifted her up. "Thou hast saved Rome, but lost thy son."

Camp
ROMAN CAMP

And so it proved, for when he had broken up his camp and returned to the Volscian territory till the senate should recall him as they proceeded, Tullus, angry and disappointed, stirred up a tumult, and he was killed by the people before he could be sent for to Rome. A temple to "Women's Good Speed" was raised on the spot where Veturia knelt to him.

Another very proud patrician family was the Quinctian. The father, Lucius Quinctius, was called Cincinnatus, from his long flowing curls of hair. He was the ablest man among the Romans, but stern and grave, and his eldest son Kæso was charged by the tribunes with a murder and fled the country. Soon after there was a great inroad of the Æqui and Volscians, and the Romans found themselves in great danger. They saw no one could save them but Cincinnatus, so they met in haste and chose him Dictator, though he was not present. Messengers were sent to his little farm on the Tiber, and there they found him holding the stilts of the plough. When they told their errand, he turned to his wife, who was helping him, and said, "Racilia, fetch me my toga;" then he washed his face and hands, and was saluted as Dictator. A boat was ready to take him to Rome, and as he landed, he was met by the four-and-twenty lictors belonging to the two consuls and escorted to his dwelling. In the morning he named as general of the cavalry Lucius Tarquitius, a brave old patrician who had become too poor even to keep a horse. Marching out at the head of all the men who could bear arms, he thoroughly routed the Æqui, and then resigned his dictatorship at the end of sixteen days. Nor would he accept any of the spoil, but went back to his plough, his only reward being that his son was forgiven and recalled from banishment.

Ploughing
PLOUGHING

These are the grand old stories that came down from old time, but how much is true no one can tell, and there is reason to think that, though the leaders like Cincinnatus and Coriolanus might be brave, the Romans were really pressed hard by the Volscians and Æqui, and lost a good deal of ground, though they were too proud to own it. No wonder, while the two orders of the state were always pulling different ways. However, the tribune Icilius succeeded in the year 454 in getting the Aventine Hill granted to the plebeians; and they had another champion called Lucius Sicinius Dentatus, who was so brave that he was called the Roman Achilles. He had received no less than forty-five wounds in different fights before he was fifty-eight years old, and had had fourteen civic crowns. For the Romans gave an oak-leaf wreath, which they called a civic crown, to a man who saved the life of a fellow-citizen, and a mural crown to him who first scaled the walls of a besieged city. And when a consul had gained a great victory, he had what was called a triumph. He was drawn in his chariot into the city, his victorious troops marching before him with their spears waving with laurel boughs, a wreath of laurel was on his head, his little children sat with him in the chariot, and the spoil of the enemy was carried along. All the people decked their houses and came forth rejoicing in holiday array, while he proceeded to the Capitol to sacrifice an ox to Jupiter there. His chief prisoners walked behind his car in chains, and at the moment of his sacrifice they were taken to a cell below the Capitol and there put to death, for the Roman was cruel in his joy. Nothing was more desired than such a triumph; but such was often the hatred between the plebeians and the patricians, that sometimes the plebeian army would stop short in the middle of a victorious campaign to hinder their consul from having a triumph. Even Sicinius is said once to have acted thus, and it began to be plain that Rome must fall if it continued to be thus divided against itself.

CHAPTER X.
THE DECEMVIRS.

B.C. 450.

The Romans began to see what mischiefs their quarrels did, and they agreed to send three of their best and wisest men to Greece to study the laws of Solon at Athens, and report whether any of them could be put in force at Rome.

To get the new code of laws which they brought home put into working order, it was agreed for the time to have no consuls, prætors, nor tribunes, but ten governors, perhaps in imitation of the nine Athenian archons. They were called Decemvirs (decem, ten; vir, a man), and at their head was Lucius Appius Claudius, the grandson of him who had killed himself to avoid being condemned for his harshness. At first they governed well, and a very good set of laws was drawn up, which the Romans called the Laws of the Ten Tables; but Appius soon began to give way to the pride of his nature, and made himself hated. There was a war with the Æqui, in which the Romans were beaten. Old Sicinius Dentatus said it was owing to bad management, and, as he had been in one hundred and twenty battles, everybody believed him. Thereupon Appius Claudius sent for him, begged for his advice, and asked him to join the army that he might assist the commanders. They received him warmly, and, when he advised them to move their camp, asked him to go and choose a place, and sent a guard with him of one hundred men. But these were really wretches instructed to kill him, and as soon as he was in a narrow rocky pass they set upon him. The brave old warrior set his back against a rock and fought so fiercely that he killed many, and the rest durst not come near him, but climbed up the rock and crushed him with stones rolled down on his head. Then they went back with a story that they had been attacked by the enemy, which was believed, till a party went out to bury the dead, and found there were only Roman corpses all lying round the crushed body of Sicinius, and that none were stripped of their armor or clothes. Then the true history was found out, but the Decemvirs sheltered the commanders, and would believe nothing against them.

Appius Claudius soon after did what horrified all honest men even more than this treachery to the brave old soldier. The Forum was not only the place of public assembly for state affairs, but the regular market-place, where there were stalls and booths for all the wares that Romans dealt in—meat stalls, wool shops, stalls where wine was sold in earthenware jars or leathern bottles, and even booths where reading and writing was taught to boys and girls, who would learn by tracing letters in the sand, and then by writing them with an iron pen on a waxen table in a frame, or with a reed upon parchment. The children of each family came escorted by a slave—the girls by their nurse, the boys by one called a pedagogue.

Virginia
DEATH OF VIRGINIA.

Appius, when going to his judgment-seat across the Forum, saw at one of these schools a girl of fifteen reading her lesson. She was so lovely that he asked her nurse who she was, and heard that her name was Virginia, and that she was the daughter of an honorable plebeian and brave centurion named Virginius, who was absent with the army fighting with the Æqui, and that she was to marry a young man named Icilius as soon as the campaign was over. Appius would gladly have married her himself, but there was a patrician law against wedding plebeians, and he wickedly determined that if he could not have her for his wife he would have her for his slave.

There was one of his clients named Marcus Claudius, whom he paid to get up a story that Virginius' wife Numitoria, who was dead, had never had any child at all, but had bought a baby of one of his slaves and had deceived her husband with it, and thus that poor Virginia was really his slave. As the maiden was reading at her school, this wretch and a band of fellows like him seized upon her, declaring that she was his property, and that he would carry her off. There was a great uproar, and she was dragged as far as Appius' judgment-seat; but by that time her faithful nurse had called the poor girl's uncle Numitorius, who could answer for it that she was really his sister's child. But Appius would not listen to him, and all that he could gain was that judgment should not be given in the matter until Virginius should have been fetched from the camp.

Races
CHARIOT RACES.

Virginius had set out from the camp with Icilius before the messengers of

Appius had reached the general with orders to stop him, and he came to the Forum leading his daughter by the hand, weeping, and attended by a great many ladies. Claudius brought his slave, who made false oath that she had sold her child to Numitoria; while, on the other hand, all the kindred of Virginius and his wife gave such proof of the contrary as any honest judge would have thought sufficient, but Appius chose to declare that the truth was with his client. There was a great murmur of all the people, but he frowned at them, and told them he knew of their meetings, and that there were soldiers in the Capitol ready to punish them, so they must stand back and not hinder a master from recovering his slave.

Virginius took his poor daughter in his arms as if to give her a last embrace, and drew her close to the stall of a butcher where lay a great knife. He wiped her tears, kissed her, and saying, "My own dear little girl, there is no way but this," he snatched up the knife and plunged it into her heart, then drawing it out he cried, "By this blood, Appius, I devote thy blood to the infernal gods."

He could not reach Appius, but the lictors could not seize him, and he mounted his horse and galloped back to the army, four hundred men following him, and he arrived still holding the knife. Every soldier who heard the story resolved no longer to bear with the Decemvirs, but to march back to the city at once and insist on the old government being restored. The Decemvir generals tried to stop them, but they only answered, "We are men with swords in our hands." At the same time there was such a tumult in the city, that Appius was forced to hide himself in his own house while Virginia's corpse was carried on a bier through the streets, and every one laid garlands, scarfs, and wreaths of their own hair upon it. When the troops arrived, they and the people joined in demanding that the Decemvirs should be given up to them to be burnt alive, and that the old magistrates should be restored. However, two patricians, Lucius Valerius and Marcus Horatius, were able so to arrange matters that the nine comparatively innocent Decemvirs were allowed to depose themselves, and Appius only was sent to prison, where he killed himself rather than face the trial that awaited him. The new code of laws, however, remained, but consuls, prætors, tribunes, and all the rest of the magistrates were restored, and in the year 445 a law was passed which enabled patricians and plebeians to intermarry.

CHAPTER XI.
CAM' BANISHMENT.

B.C. 390.

The wars with the Etruscans went on, and chiefly with the city of Veii, which stood on a hill twelve miles from Rome, and was altogether thirty years at war with it. At last the Romans made up their minds that, instead of going home every harvest-time to gather in their crops, they must watch the city constantly till they could take it, and thus, as the besiegers were unable to do their own work, pay was raised for them to enable them to get it done, and this was the beginning of paying armies.

Machine
ARROW MACHINE.

The siege of Veii lasted ten years, and during the last the Alban lake filled to an unusual height, although the summer was very dry. One of the Veian soldiers cried out to the Romans half in jest, "You will never take Veii till the Alban lake is dry." It turned out that there was an old tradition that Veii should fall when the lake was drained. On this the senate sent orders to have canals dug to carry the waters to the sea, and these still remain. Still Veii held out, and to finish the war a dictator was appointed, Marcus Furius Cam, who chose for his second in command a man of one of the most virtuous families in Rome, as their surname testified, Publius Cornelius, called Scipio, or the Staff, because either he or one of his forefathers had been the staff of his father's old age. Cam took the city by assault, with an immense quantity of spoil, which was divided among the soldiers.

Cam in his pride took to himself at his triumph honors that had hitherto only been paid to the gods. He had his face painted with vermilion and his car drawn by milk-white horses. This shocked the people, and he gave greater offence by declaring that he had vowed a tenth part of the spoil to Apollo, but had forgotten it in the division of the plunder, and now must take it again. The soldiers would not consent, but lest the god should be angry with them, it was resolved to send a gold vase to his oracle at Delphi. All the women of Rome brought their jewels, and the senate rewarded them by a decree that funeral speeches might be made over their graves as over those of men, and likewise that they might be driven in chariots to the public games.

Cam commanded in another war with the Falisci, also an Etruscan race, and laid siege to their city. The sons of almost all the chief families were in charge of a sort of schoolmaster, who taught them both reading and all kinds of exercises. One day this man, pretending to take the boys out walking, led them all into the enemy's camp, to the tent of Cam, where he told that he brought them all, and with them the place, since the Romans had only to threaten their lives to make their fathers deliver up the city. Cam, however, was so shocked at such perfidy, that he immediately bade the lictors strip the fellow instantly, and give the boys rods with which to scourge him back into the town. Their fathers were so grateful that they made peace at once, and about the same time the Æqui were also conquered; and the commons and open lands belonging to Veii being divided, so that each Roman freeman had six acres, the plebeians were contented for the time.

machine
SIEGE MACHINE

The truth seems to have been that these Etruscan nations were weakened by a great new nation coming on them from the North. They were what the Romans called Galli or Gauls, one of the great races of the old stock which has always been finding its way westward into Europe, and they had their home north of the Alps, but they were always pressing on and on, and had long since made settlements in northern Italy. They were in clans, each obedient to one chief as a father, and joining together in one brotherhood. They had lands to which whole families had a common right, and when their numbers outgrew what the land could maintain, the bolder ones would set off with their wives, children, and cattle to find new homes. The Greeks and Romans themselves had begun first in the same way, and their tribes, and the claims of all to the common land, were the remains of the old way; but they had been settled in cities so long that this had been forgotten, and they were very different people from the wild men who spoke what we call Welsh, and wore checked tartan trews and plaids, with gold collars round their necks, round shields, huge broadswords, and their red or black hair long and shaggy. The Romans knew little or nothing about what passed beyond their own Apennines, and went on with their own quarrels. Cam was accused of having taken more than his proper share of the spoil of Veii, in especial a brass door from a temple. His friends offered to pay any fine that might be laid on him, but he was too proud to stand his trial, and chose rather to leave Rome. As he passed the gates, he turned round and called upon the gods to bring Rome to speedy repentance for having driven him away.

Even then the Gauls were in the midst of a war with Clusium, the city of Porsena, and the inhabitants sent to beg the help of the Romans, and the senate sent three young brothers of the Fabian family to try to arrange matters. They met the Gaulish Bran or chief, whom Latin authors call Brennus, and asked him what was his quarrel with Clusium or his right to any part of Etruria. Brennus answered that his right was his sword, and that all things belonged to the brave, and that his quarrel with the men of Clusium was, that though they had more land than they could till, they would not yield him any. As to the Romans, they had robbed their neighbors already, and had no right to find fault.

This put the Fabian brothers in a rage, and they forgot the caution of their family, as well as those rules of all nations which forbid an ambassador to fight, and also forbid his person to be touched by the enemy; and when the men of Clusium made an attack on the Gauls they joined in the attack, and Quintus, the eldest brother, slew one of the chiefs. Brennus, wild as he was, knew these laws of nations, and in great anger broke up his siege of Clusium, and, marching towards Rome, demanded that the Fabii should be given up to him. Instead of this, the Romans made them all three military tribunes, and as the Gauls came nearer the whole army marched out to meet them in such haste that they did not wait to sacrifice to the gods nor consult the omens. The tribunes were all young and hot-headed, and they despised the Gauls; so out they went to attack them on the banks of the Allia, only seven and a-half miles from Rome. A most terrible defeat they had; many fell in the field, many were killed in the flight, others were drowned in trying to swim the Tiber, others scattered to Veii and the other cities, and a few, horror-stricken and wet through, rushed into Rome with the sad tidings. There were not men enough left to defend the walls! The enemy would instantly be upon them! The only place strong enough to keep them out was the Capitol, and that would only hold a few people within it! So there was nothing for it but flight. The braver, stronger men shut themselves up in the Capitol; all the rest, with the women and children, put their most precious goods into carts and left the city. The Vestal Virgins carried the sacred fire, and were plodding along in the heat, when a plebeian named Albinus saw their state, helped them into his cart, and took them to the city of Cumæ, where they found shelter in a temple. And so Rome was left to the enemy.

CHAPTER XII.
THE SACK OF ROME.

B.C. 390.

Rome was left to the enemy, except for the small garrison in the Capitol and for eighty of the senators, men too old to flee, who devoted themselves to the gods to save the rest, and, arraying themselves in their robes—some as former consuls, some as priests, some as generals—sat down with their ivory staves in their hands, in their chairs of state in the Forum, to await the enemy.

Forum
RUINS OF THE FORUM AT ROME.

In burst the savage Gauls, roaming all over the city till they came to the Forum, where they stood amazed and awe-struck at the sight of the eighty grand old men motionless in their chairs. At first they looked at the strange, calm figures as if they were the gods of the place, until one Gaul, as if desirous of knowing whether they were flesh and blood or not, stroked the beard of the nearest. The senator, esteeming this an insult, struck the man on the face with his staff, and this was the sign for the slaughter of them all.

Then the Gauls began to plunder every house, dragging out and killing the few inhabitants they found there; feasting, revelling, and piling up riches to carry away; burning and overthrowing the houses. Day after day the little garrison in the Capitol saw the sight, and wondered if their stock of food would hold out till the Gauls should go away or till their friends should come to their relief. Yet when the day came round for the sacrifice to the ancestor of one of these beleaguered men, he boldly went forth to the altar of his own ruined house on the Quirinal Hill, and made his offering to his forefathers, nor did one Gaul venture to touch him, seeing that he was performing a religious rite.

The escaped Romans had rested at Ardea, where they found Cam, and were by him formed into an army, but he would not take the generalship without authority from what was left of the Senate, and that was shut up in the Capitol in the midst of the Gauls. A brave man, however, named Pontius Cominius, declared that he could make his way through the Gauls by night, and climb up the Capitol and down again by a precipice which they did not watch because they thought no one could mount it, and that he would bring back the orders of the Senate. He swam the Tiber by the help of corks, landed at night in ruined Rome among the sleeping enemy, and climbed up the rock, bringing hope at last to the worn-out and nearly starving garrison. Quickly they met, recalled the sentence of banishment against Cam, and named him Dictator. Pontius, having rested in the meantime, slid down the rock and made his way back to Ardea safely; but the broken twigs and torn ivy on the rock showed the Gauls that it had been scaled, and they resolved that where man had gone man could go. So Brennus told off the most surefooted mountaineers he could find, and at night, two and two, they crept up the crag, so silently that no alarm was given, till just as they came to the top, some geese that were kept as sacred to Juno, and for that reason had been spared in spite of the scarcity, began to scream and cackle, and thus brought to the spot a brave officer called Marcus Manlius, who found two Gauls in the act of setting foot on the level ground on the top. With a sweep of his sword he struck off the hand of one, and with his buckler smote the other on the head, tumbling them both headlong down, knocking down their fellows in their flight, and the Capitol was saved.

By way of reward every Roman soldier brought Manlius a few grains of the corn he received from the common stock and a few drops of wine, while the tribune who was on guard that night was thrown from the rock.

Foiled thus, and with great numbers of his men dying from the fever that always prevailed in Rome in summer, Brennus thought of retreating, and offered to leave Rome if the garrison in the Capitol would pay him a thousand pounds' weight of gold. There was treasure enough in the temples to do this, and as they could not tell what Cam was about, nor if Pontius had reached him safely, and they were on the point of being starved, they consented. The gold was brought to the place appointed by the Gauls, and when the weights proved not to be equal to the amount that the Romans had with them, Brennus resolved to have all, put his sword into the other scale, saying, "Væ victis"—"Woe to the conquered." But at that moment there was a noise outside —Cam was come. The Gauls were cut down and slain among the ruins, those who fled were killed by the people in the country as they wandered in the fields, and not one returned to tell the tale. So the ransom of the Capitol was rescued, and was laid up by Cam in the vaults as a reserve for future danger.

This was the Roman story, but their best historians say that it is made better for Rome than is quite the truth, for that the Capitol was really conquered, and the Gauls helped themselves to whatever they chose and went off with it, though sickness and weariness made them afterwards disperse, so that they were mostly cut off by the country people.

Every old record had been lost and destroyed, so that, before this, Roman history can only be hearsay, derived from what the survivors recollected; and the whole of the buildings, temples, senate-house, and dwellings lay in ruins. Some of the citizens wished to change the site of the city to Veii; but Cam, who was Dictator, was resolved to hold fast by the hearths of their fathers, and while the debate was going on in the ruins of the senate-house a troop of soldiers were marching in, and the centurion was heard calling out, "Plant your ensign here; this is a good place to stay in." "A happy omen," cried one of the senators; "I adore the gods who gave it." So it was settled to rebuild the city, and in digging among the ruins there were found the golden rod of Romulus, the brazen tables on which the Laws of the Twelve Tables were engraved, and other brasses with records of treaties with other nations. Fabius was accused of having done all the harm by having broken the law of nations, but he was spared at the entreaty of his friends. Manlius was surnamed Capitolinus, and had a house granted him on the Capitol; and Cam when he laid down his dictatorship, was saluted as like Romulus—another founder of Rome.

The new buildings were larger and more ornamented than the old ones; but the lines of the old underground drains, built in the mighty Etruscan fashion by the elder Tarquin as it was said, were not followed, and this tended to render Rome more unhealthy, so that few of her richer citizens lived there in summer or autumn, but went out to country houses on the hills.

forum
ENTRY OF THE FORUM ROMANUM BY THE VIA SACRA

CHAPTER XIII.
THE PLEBEIAN CONSULATE.

B.C. 367.

All the old enemies of Rome attacked her again when she was weak and rising out of her ruins, but Cam had wisely persuaded the Romans to add the people of Veii, Capena, and Falerii to the number of their citizens, making four more tribes; and this addition to their numbers helped them beat off their foes.

But this enlarged the number of the plebeians, and enabled them to make their claims more heard. Moreover, the old quarrel between poor and rich, debtor and creditor, broke out again. Those who had saved their treasure in the time of the sack had made loans to those who had lost to enable them to build their houses and stock their farms again, and after a time they called loudly for payment, and when it was not forthcoming had the debtors seized to be sold as slaves. Cam himself was one of the hardest creditors of all, and the barracks where slaves were placed to be sold were full of citizens.

costumes
COSTUMES.

Marcus Manlius Capitolinus was full of pity, and raised money to redeem four hundred of them, trying with all his might to get the law changed and to save the rest; but the rich men and the patricians thought he acted only out of jealousy of Cam, and to get up a party for himself. They said he was raising a sedition, and Publius Cornelius Cossus was named Dictator to put it down. Manlius was seized and put into chains, but released again. At last the rich men bought over two of the tribunes to accuse him of wanting to make himself a king, and this hated title turned all the people against their friend, so that the general cry sentenced him to be cast down from the top of the Tarpeian rock; his house on the Capitol was overthrown, and his family declared that no son of their house should ever again bear the name of Manlius.

costume
COSTUME.

Yet the plebeians were making their way, and at last succeeded in gaining the plebeian magistracies and equal honors with the patricians. A curious story is told of the cause of the last effort which gained the day. A patrician named Fabius Ambustus had two daughters, one of whom he gave in marriage to Servius Sulpicius, a patrician and military tribune, the other to Licinius Stolo. One day, when Stolo's wife was visiting her sister, there was a great noise and thundering at the gates which frightened her, until the other Fabii said it was only her husband coming home from the Forum attended by his lictors and clients, laughing at her ignorance and alarm, until a whole troop of the clients came in to pay their court to the tribune's wife.

Stolo's wife went home angry and vexed, and reproached her husband and her father for not having made her equal with her sister, and so wrought on them that they put themselves at the head of the movement in favor of the plebeians; and Licinius and another young plebeian named Lucius Sextius, being elected year after year tribunes of the people, went on every time saying Veto to whatever was proposed by anybody, and giving out that they should go on doing so till three measures were carried—viz., that interest on debt should not be demanded; that no citizen should possess more than three hundred and twenty acres of the public land, or feed more than a certain quantity of cattle on the public pastures; and, lastly, that one of the two consuls should always be a plebeian.

They went on for eight years, always elected by the people and always stopping everything. At last there was another inroad of the Gauls expected, and Cam, though eighty years old, was for the fifth time chosen Dictator, and gained a great victory upon the banks of the Anio. The Senate begged him to continue Dictator till he could set their affairs to rights, and he vowed to build a temple to Concord if he could succeed. He saw indeed that it was time to yield, and persuaded the Senate to think so; so that at last, in the year 367, Sextius was elected consul, together with a patrician, Æmilius. Even then the Senate would not receive Sextius till he was introduced by Cam. From this time the patricians and plebeians were on an equal footing as far as regarded the magistracies, but the priesthood could belong only to the patricians. Cam lived to a great age, and was honored as having three times saved his country. He died at last of a terrible pestilence which raged in Rome in the year 365.

The priests recommended that they should invite the players from Etruria to perform a drama in honor of the feats of the gods, and this was the beginning of play-acting in Rome.

Not long after there yawned a terrible chasm in the Forum, most likely from an earthquake, but nothing seemed to fill it up, and the priests and augurs consulted their oracles about it. These made answer that it would only close on receiving of what was most precious. Gold and jewels were thrown in, but it still seemed bottomless, and at last the augurs declared that it was courage that was the most precious thing in Rome. Thereupon a patrician youth named Marcus Curtius decked himself in his choicest robes, put on his armor, took his shield, sword, and spear, mounted his horse, and leapt headlong into the gulf, thus giving it the most precious of all things, courage and self-devotion.

After this one story says it closed of itself, another that it became easy to fill it up with earth.

The Romans thought that such a sacrifice must please the gods and bring them success in their battles; but in the war with the Hernici that was now being waged the plebeian consul was killed, and no doubt there was much difficulty in getting the patricians to obey a plebeian properly, for in the course of the next twenty years it was necessary fourteen times to appoint a Dictator for the defence of the state, so that it is plain there must have been many alarms and much difficulty in enforcing discipline; but, on the whole, success was with Rome, and the neighboring tribes grew weaker.

curtius
CURTIUS LEAPING INTO THE GULF. (From a Bas-Relief.)

CHAPTER XIV.
THE DEVOTION OF DECIUS.

B.C. 357

Other tribes of the Gauls did not fail to come again and make fresh inroads on the valleys of the Tiber and Anio. Whenever they came, instead of choosing men from the tribes to form an army, as in a war with their neighbors, all the fighting men of the nation turned out to oppose them, generally under a Dictator.

In one of these wars the Gauls came within three miles of Rome, and the two hosts were encamped on the banks of the Anio, with a bridge between them. Along this bridge strutted an enormous Gallic chief, much taller than any of the Romans, boasting himself, and calling on any one of them to come out and fight with him. Again it was a Manlius who distinguished himself. Titus, a young man of that family, begged the Dictator's permission to accept the challenge, and, having gained it, he changed his round knight's shield for the square one of the foot soldiers, and with his short sword came forward on the bridge. The Gaul made a sweep at him with his broadsword, but, slipping within the guard, Manlius stabbed the giant in two places, and as he fell cut off his head, and took the torc, or broad twisted gold collar that was the mark of all Gallic chieftains. Thence the brave youth was called Titus Manlius Torquatus—a surname to make up for that of Capitolinus, which had never been used again.

appenines
THE APENNINES.

The next time the Gauls came, Marcus Valerius, a descendant of the old hero Publicola, was consul, and gained a great victory. It was said that in the midst of the fight a monstrous raven appeared flying over his head, resting now and then on his helmet, but generally pecking at the eyes of the Gauls and flapping its wings in their faces, so that they fled discomfited. Thence he was called Corvus or Corvinus. The Gauls never again came in such force, but a new enemy came against them, namely, the Samnites, a people who dwelt to the south of them. They were of Italian blood, mountaineers of the Southern Apennines, not unlike the Romans in habits, language, and training, and the staunchest enemies they had yet encountered. The war began from an entreaty from the people of Campania to the Romans to defend them from the attacks of the Samnites. For the Campanians, living in the rich plains, whose name is still unchanged, were an idle, languid people, whom the stout men of Samnium could easily overcome. The Romans took their part, and Valerius Corvus gained a victory at Mount Gaurus; but the other consul, Cornelius Cossus, fell into danger, having marched foolishly into a forest, shut in by mountains, and with only one way out through a deep valley, which was guarded by the Samnites. In this almost hopeless danger one of the military tribunes, Publius Decius Mus, discovered a little hill above the enemy's camp, and asked leave to lead a small body of men to seize it, since he would be likely thus to draw off the Samnites, and while they were destroying him, as he fully expected, the Romans could get out of the valley. Hidden by the wood, he gained the hill, and there the Samnites saw him, to their great amazement; and while they were considering whether to attack him, the other Romans were able to march out of the valley. Finding he was not attacked, Decius set guards, and, when night came on, marched down again as quietly as possible to join the army, who were now on the other side of the Samnite camp. Through the midst of this he and his little camp went without alarm, until, about half-way across, one Roman struck his foot against a shield. The noise awoke the Samnites, but Decius caused his men to give a great shout, and this, in the darkness, so confused the enemy that they missed the little body of Romans, who safely gained their own camp. Decius cut short the thanks and joy of the consul by advising him to fall at once on the Samnite camp in its dismay, and this was done; the Samnites were entirely routed, 30,000 killed, and their camp taken. Decius received for his reward a hundred oxen, a white bull with gilded horns, and three crowns—one of gold for courage, one of oak for having saved the lives of his fellow-citizens, and one of grass for having taken the enemy's camp—while all his men were for life to receive a double allowance of corn. Decius offered up the white bull in sacrifice to Mars, and gave the oxen to the companions of his glory.

Afterwards Valerius routed the Samnites again, and his troops brought in 120 standards and 40,000 shields which they had picked up, having been thrown away by the enemy in their flight.

Peace was made for the time; but the Latins, now in alliance with Rome, began to make war on the Samnites. They complained, and the Romans feeling bound to take their part, a great Latin war began. Manlius Torquatus and Decius Mus, the two greatest heroes of Rome, were consuls. As the Latins and Romans were alike in dress, arms, and language, in order to prevent taking friend for foe, strict orders were given that no one should attack a Latin without orders, or go out of his rank, on pain of death. A Latin champion came out boasting, as the two armies lay beneath Mount Vesuvius, then a fair vine-clad hill showing no flame. Young Manlius remembering his father's fame, darted out, fought hand to hand with the Latin, slew him, and brought home his spoils to his father's feet. He had forgotten that his father had only fought after permission was given. The elder Manlius received him with stern grief. He had broken the law of discipline, and he must die. His head was struck off amid the grief and anger of the army. The battle was bravely fought, but it went against the Romans at first. Then Decius, recollecting a vision which had declared that a consul must devote himself for his country, called on Valerius, the Pontifex Maximus, to dedicate him. He took off his armor, put on his purple toga, covered his head with a veil, and standing on a spear, repeated the words of consecration after Valerius, then mounted his horse and rode in among the Latins. They at first made way, but presently closed in and overpowered him with a shower of darts; and thus he gave for his country the life he had once offered for it.

The victory was won, and was so followed up that the Latins were forced to yield to Rome. Some of the cities retained their own laws and magistrates, but others had Romans with their families settled in them, and were called colonies, while the Latin people themselves became Roman citizens in everything but the power of becoming magistrates or voting for them, being, in fact, very much what the earliest plebeians had been before they acquired any rights.

CHAPTER XV.
THE SAMNITE WARS.

In the year 332, just when Alexander the Great was making his conquests in the East, his uncle Alexander, king of Epirus, brother to his mother Olympius, came to Italy, where there were so many Grecian citizens south of the Samnites that the foot of Italy was called Magna Græcia, or Greater Greece. He attacked the Samnites, and the Romans were not sorry to see them weakened, and made an alliance with him. He stayed in Italy about six years, and was then killed.

To overthrow the Samnites was the great object of Rome at this time, and for this purpose they offered their protection and alliance to all the cities that stood in dread of that people. One of the cities was founded by men from the isle of Euboea, who called it Neapolis, or the New City, to distinguish it from the old town near at hand, which they called Palæopolis, or the Old City. The elder city held out against the Romans, but was easily overpowered, while the new one submitted to Rome; but these southern people were very shallow and fickle, and little to be depended on, as they often changed sides between the Romans and Samnites. In the midst of the siege of Palæopolis, the year of the consulate came to an end, but the Senate, while causing two consuls as usual to be elected, at home, would not recall Publilius Philo from the siege, and therefore appointed him proconsul there. This was in 326, and was the beginning of the custom of sending the ex-consul as proconsul to command the armies or govern the provinces at a distance from home.

samnites
COMBAT BETWEEN A MIRMILLO AND A SAMNITE.

samnite
COMBAT BETWEEN A LIGHT-ARMED GLADIATOR AND A SAMNITE.

In 320, the consul falling sick, a dictator was appointed, Lucius Papirius Cursor, one of the most stern and severe men in Rome. He was obliged by some religious ceremony to return to Rome for a time, and he forbade his lieutenant, Quintus Fabius Rullianus, to venture a battle in his absence. But so good an opportunity offered that Fabius attacked the enemy, beat them, and killed 20,000 men. Then selfishly unwilling to have the spoils he had won carried in the dictator's triumph, he burnt them all. Papirius arrived in great anger, and sentenced him to death for his disobedience; but while the lictors were stripping him, he contrived to escape from their hands among the soldiers, who closed on him, so that he was able to get to Rome, where his father called the Senate together, and they showed themselves so resolved to save his life that Papirius was forced to pardon him, though not without reproaching the Romans for having fallen from the stern justice of Brutus and Manlius.

Two years later the two consuls, Titus Veturius and Spurius Posthumius, were marching into Campania, when the Samnite commander, Pontius Herennius, sent forth people disguised as shepherds to entice them into a narrow mountain pass near the city of Candium, shut in by thick woods, leading into a hollow curved valley, with thick brushwood on all sides, and only one way out, which the Samnites blocked up with trunks of trees. As soon as the Romans were within this place the other end was blocked in the same way, and thus they were all closed up at the mercy of their enemies.

What was to be done with them? asked the Samnites; and they went to consult old Herennius, the father of Pontius, the wisest man in the nation. "Open the way and let them all go free," he said.

"What! without gaining any advantage?"

"Then kill them all."

He was asked to explain such extraordinary advice. He said that to release them generously would be to make them friends and allies for ever; but if the war was to go on, the best thing for Samnium would be to destroy such a number of enemies at a blow. But the Samnites could not resolve upon either plan; so they took a middle course, the worst of all, since it only made the Romans furious without weakening them. They were made to take off all their armor and lay down their weapons, and thus to pass out under the yoke, namely, three spears set up like a doorway. The consuls, after agreeing to a disgraceful peace, had to go first, wearing only their undermost garment, then all the rest, two and two, and if any one of them gave an angry look, he was immediately knocked down and killed. They went on in silence into Campania, where, when night came on, they all threw themselves, half-naked, silent, and hungry upon the grass. The people of Capua came out to help them, and brought them food and clothing, trying to do them all honor and comfort them, but they would neither look up nor speak. And thus they went on to Rome, where everybody had put on mourning, and all the ladies went without their jewels, and the shops in the Forum were closed. The unhappy men stole into their houses at night one by one, and the consuls would not resume their office, but two were appointed to serve instead for the rest of the year.

rome
ANCIENT ROME.

Revenge was all that was thought of, but the difficulty was the peace to which the consuls had sworn. Posthumius said that if it was disavowed by the Senate, he, who had been driven to make it, must be given back to the Samnites. So, with his hands tied, he was taken back to the Samnite camp by a herald and delivered over; but at that moment Posthumius gave the herald a kick, crying out, "I am now a Samnite, and have insulted you, a Roman herald. This is a just cause of war." Pontius and the Samnites were very angry, and they said it was an unworthy trick; but they did not prevent Posthumius from going safely back to the Romans, who considered him to have quite retrieved his honor.

A battle was fought, in which Pontius and 7000 men were forced to lay down their arms and pass under the yoke in their turn. The struggle between these two fierce nations lasted altogether seventy years, and the Romans had many defeats. They had other wars at the same time. They never subdued Etruria, and in the battle of Sentinum, fought with the Gauls, the consul Decius Mus, devoted himself exactly as his father had done at Vesuvius, and by his death won the victory.

The Samnite wars may be considered as ending in 290, when the chief general of Samnium, Pontius Telesimus, was made prisoner and put to death at Rome. The lands in the open country were quite subdued, but many Samnites still lived in the fastnesses of the Apennines in the south, which have ever since been the haunt of wild untamed men.

CHAPTER XVI.
THE WAR WITH PYRRHUS.

B.C. 280-271.

In the Grecian History you remember that Pyrrhus, king of Epirus, the townsman of Alexander the Great, made an expedition to Italy. This was the way it came about. The city of Tarentum was a Spartan colony at the head of the gulf that bears its name. It was as proud as its parent, but had lost all the grave sternness of manners, and was as idle and fickle as the other places in that languid climate. The Tarentines first maltreated some Roman ships which put into their gulf, and then insulted the ambassador who was sent to complain. Then when the terrible Romans were found to be really coming to revenge their honor, the Tarentines took fright, and sent to beg Pyrrhus to come to their aid.

He readily accepted the invitation, and coming to Italy with 28,000 men and twenty elephants, hoped to conquer the whole country; but he found the Tarentines not to be trusted, and soon weary of entertaining him, while they could not keep their promises of aid from the other Greeks of Italy.

pyrrhus
PYRRHUS.

The Romans marched against him, and there was a great battle on the banks of the river Siris, where the fighting was very hard, but when the elephants charged the Romans broke and fled, and were only saved by nightfall from being entirely destroyed. So great, however, had been Pyrrhus' loss that he said, "Such another victory, and I shall have to go back alone to Epirus."

He thought he had better treat with the Romans, and sent his favorite counsellor Kineas to offer to make peace, provided the Romans would promise safety to his Italian allies, and presents were sent to the senators and their wives to induce them to listen favorably. People in ancient Greece expected such gifts to back a suit; but Kineas found that nobody in Rome would hear of being bribed, though many were not unwilling to make peace. Blind old Appius Claudius, who had often been consul, caused himself to be led into the Senate to oppose it, for it was hard to his pride to make peace as defeated men. Kineas was much struck with Rome, where he found a state of things like the best days of Greece, and, going back to his master, told him that the senate-house was like a temple, and those who sat there like an assembly of kings, and that he feared they were fighting with the Hydra of Lerna, for as soon as they had destroyed one Roman army another had sprung up in its place.

However, the Romans wanted to treat about the prisoners Pyrrhus had taken, and they sent Caius Fabricius to the Greek camp for the purpose. Kineas reported him to be a man of no wealth, but esteemed as a good soldier and an honest man. Pyrrhus tried to make him take large presents, but nothing would Fabricius touch; and then, in the hope of alarming him, in the middle of a conversation the hangings of one side of the tent suddenly fell, and disclosed the biggest of all the elephants, who waved his trunk over Fabricius and trumpeted frightfully. The Roman quietly turned round and smiled as he said to the king, "I am no more moved by your gold than by your great beast."

orator
ROMAN ORATOR.

At supper there was a conversation on Greek philosophy, of which the Romans as yet knew nothing. When the doctrine of Epicurus was mentioned, that man's life was given to be spent in the pursuit of joy, Fabricius greatly amused the company by crying out, "O Hercules! grant that the Greeks may be heartily of this mind so long as we have to fight with them."

Pyrrhus even tried to persuade Fabricius to enter his service, but the answer was, "Sir. I advise you not; for if your people once tasted of my rule, they would all desire me to govern them instead of you." Pyrrhus consented to let the prisoners go home, but, if no peace were made, they were to return again as soon as the Saturnalia were over; and this was faithfully done. Fabricius was consul the next year, and thus received a letter from Pyrrhus' physician, offering for a reward to rid the Romans of his master by poison. The two consuls sent it to the king with the following letter:—"Caius Fabricius and Quintus Æmilius, consuls, to Pyrrhus, king, greeting. You choose your friends and foes badly. This letter will show that you make war with honest men and trust rogues and knaves. We tell you, not to win your favor, but lest your ruin might bring on the reproach of ending the war by treachery instead of force."

Pyrrhus made enquiry, put the physician to death, and by way of acknowledgment released the captives, trying again to make peace; but the Romans would accept no terms save that he should give up the Tarentines and go back in the same ships. A battle was fought in the wood of Asculum. Decius Mus declared he would devote himself like his father and grandfather; but Pyrrhus heard of this, and sent word that he had given orders that Decius should not be killed, but taken alive and scourged; and this prevented him. The Romans were again forced back by the might of the elephants, but not till night fell on them. Pyrrhus had been wounded, and hosts of Greeks had fallen, among them many of Pyrrhus' chief friends.

He then went to Sicily, on an invitation from the Greeks settled there, to defend them from the Carthaginians; but finding them as little satisfactory as the Italian Greeks, he suddenly came back to Tarentum. This time one of the consuls was Marcus Curius—called Dentatus, because he had been born with teeth in his mouth—a stout, plain old Roman, very stern, for when he levied troops against Pyrrhus, the first man who refused to serve was punished by having his property seized and sold. He then marched southward, and at Beneventum at length entirely defeated Pyrrhus, and took four of his elephants. Pyrrhus was obliged to return to Epirus, and the Roman steadiness had won the day after nine years.

Dentatus had the grandest triumph that had ever been known at Rome, with the elephants walking in the procession, the first that the Romans had ever seen. All the spoil was given up to the commonwealth; and when, some time after, it was asserted that he had taken some for himself, it turned out that he had only kept one old wooden vessel, which he used in sacrificing to the gods.

The Greeks of Southern Italy had behaved very ill to Pyrrhus and turned against him. The Romans found them so fickle and troublesome that they were all reduced in one little war after another. The Tarentines had to surrender and lose their walls and their fleet, and so had the people of Sybaris, who have become a proverb for idleness, for they were so lazy that they were said to have killed all their crowing-birds for waking them too early in the morning. All the peninsula of Italy now belonged to Rome, and great roads were made of paved stones connecting them with it, many of which remain to this day, even the first of all, called the Appian Way, from Rome to Capua, which was made under the direction of the censor Appius Claudius, during the Samnite war.

CHAPTER XVII.
THE FIRST PUNIC WAR.

We are now come to the time when Rome became mixed up in wars with nations beyond Italy. There was a great settlement of the Phoenicians, the merchants of the old world, at Carthage, on the northern coast of Africa, the same place at which Virgil afterwards described Æneas as spending so much time. Dido, the queen who was said to have founded Carthage when fleeing from her wicked brother-in-law at Tyre, is thought to have been an old goddess, and the religion and manners of the Carthaginians were thoroughly Phoenician, or, as the Romans called them, Punic. They had no king, but a Senate, and therewith rulers called by the name that is translated as judges in the Bible; and they did not love war, only trade, and spread out their settlements for this purpose all over the coast of the Mediterranean, from Spain to the Black Sea, wherever a country had mines, wool, dyes, spices, or men to trade with; and their sailors were the boldest to be found anywhere, and were the only ones who had passed beyond the Pillars of Hercules, namely, the Straits of Gibraltar, in the Atlantic Ocean. They built handsome cities, and country houses with farms and gardens round them, and had all tokens of wealth and luxury—ivory, jewels, and spices from India, pearls from the Persian Gulf, gold from Spain, silver from the Balearic Isles, tin from the Scilly Isles, amber from the Baltic; and they had forts to protect their settlements. They generally hired the men of the countries, where they settled, to fight their battles, sometimes under hired Greek captains, but often under generals of their own.

ship
ROMAN SHIP.

The first place where they did not have everything their own way was Sicily. The old inhabitants of the island were called Sicels, a rough people; but besides these there were a great number of Greek settlements, also of Carthaginian ones, and these two hated one another. The Carthaginians tried to overthrow the Greeks, and Pyrrhus, by coming to help his countrymen, only made them more bitter against one another. When he went away he exclaimed, "What an arena we leave for the Romans and Carthaginians to contend upon!" so sure was he that these two great nations must soon fight out the struggle for power.

The beginning of the struggle was, however, brought on by another cause. Messina, the place founded long ago by the brave exiles of Messene, when the Spartans had conquered their state, had been seized by a troop of Mamertines, fierce Italians from Mamertum; and these, on being threatened by Xiero, king of Syracuse, sent to offer to become subjects to the Romans, thus giving them the command of the port which secured the entrance of the island. The Senate had great scruples about accepting the offer, and supporting a set of mere robbers; but the two consuls and all the people could not withstand the temptation, and it was resolved to assist the Mamertines. Thus began what was called the First Punic War. The difficulty was, however, want of ships. The Romans had none of their own, and though they collected a few from their Greek allies in Italy, it was not in time to prevent some of the Mamertines from surrendering the citadel to Xanno, the Carthaginian general, who thought himself secure, and came down to treat with the Roman tribune Claudius, haughtily bidding the Romans no more to try to meddle with the sea, for they should not be allowed so much as to wash their hands in it. Claudius, angered at this, treacherously laid hands on Xanno, and he agreed to give up the castle on being set free; but he had better have remained a prisoner, for the Carthaginians punished him with crucifixion, and besieged Messina, but in vain.

The Romans felt that a fleet was necessary, and set to work to build war galleys on the pattern of a Carthaginian one which had been wrecked upon their coast. While a hundred ships were building, oarsmen were trained to row on dry land, and in two months the fleet put to sea. Knowing that there was no chance of being able to fight according to the regular rules of running the beaks of their galleys into the sides of those of their enemies, they devised new plans of letting heavy weights descend on the ships of the opposite fleet, and then of letting drawbridges down by which to board them. The Carthaginians, surprised and dismayed, when thus attacked off Mylæ by the consul Duilius, were beaten and chased to Sardinia, where their unhappy commander was nailed to a cross by his own soldiers; while Duilius not only received in Rome a grand triumph for his first naval victory, but it was decreed that he should never go out into the city at night without a procession of torch-bearers.

The Romans now made up their minds to send an expedition to attack the Carthaginian power not only in Sicily but in Africa, and this was placed under the command of a sturdy plebeian consul, Marcus Attilius Regulus. He fought a great battle with the Carthaginian fleet on his way, and he had even more difficulty with his troops, who greatly dreaded the landing in Africa as a place of unknown terror. He landed, however, at some distance from the city, and did not at once advance on it. When he did, according to the story current at Rome, he encountered on the banks of the River Bagrada an enormous serpent, whose poisonous breath killed all who approached it, and on whose scales darts had no effect. At last the machines for throwing huge stones against city walls were used against it; its backbone was broken, and it was at last killed, and its skin sent to Rome.

The Romans met other enemies, whom they defeated, and gained much plunder. The Senate, understanding that the Carthaginians were cooped up within their walls, recalled half the army. Regulus wished much to return, as the slave who tilled his little farm had run away with his plough, and his wife was in distress; but he was so valuable that he could not be recalled, and he remained and soon took Tunis. The Carthaginians tried to win their gods' favor back by offering horrid human sacrifices to Moloch and Baal, and then hired a Spartan general named Xanthippus, who defeated the Romans, chiefly by means of the elephants, and made Regulus prisoner. The Romans, who hated the Carthaginians so much as to believe them capable of any wickedness, declared that in their jealousy of Xanthippus' victory, they sent him home to Greece in a vessel so arranged as to founder at sea.

battle
ROMAN ORDER OF BATTLE.

However, the Romans, after several disasters in Sicily, gained a great victory near Panormus, capturing one hundred elephants, which were brought to Rome to be hunted by the people that they might lose their fear of them. The Carthaginians were weakened enough to desire peace, and they sent Regulus to propose it, making him swear to return if he did not succeed. He came to the outskirts of the city, but would not enter. He said he was no Roman proconsul, but the slave of Carthage. However, the Senate came out to hear him, and he gave the message, but added that the Romans ought not to accept these terms, but to stand out for much better ones, giving such reasons that the whole people was persuaded. He was entreated to remain and not meet the angry men of Carthage; but nothing would persuade him to break his word, and he went back. The Romans told dreadful stories of the treatment he met with—how his eyelids were cut off and he was put in the sunshine, and at last he was nailed up in a barrel lined with spikes and rolled down hill. Some say that this was mere report, and that Carthaginian prisoners at Rome were as savagely treated; but at any rate the constancy of Regulus has always been a proverb.

The war went on, and one of the proud Claudius family was in command at Trepanum, in Sicily, when the enemy's fleet came in sight. Before a battle the Romans always consulted the sacred fowls that were carried with the army. Claudius was told that their augury was against a battle—they would not eat. "Then let them drink," he cried, and threw them into the sea. His impiety, as all felt it, was punished by an utter defeat, and he killed himself to avoid an enquiry. The war went on by land and sea all over and around Sicily, till at the end of twenty-four years peace was made, just after another great sea-fight, in which Rome had the victory. She made the Carthaginians give up all they held in Sicily, restore their prisoners, make a large payment, and altogether humble their claims; thus beginning a most bitter hatred towards the conquerors, who as greatly hated and despised them. Thus ended the First Punic War.

CHAPTER XVIII.
CONQUEST OF CISALPINE GAUL.

240-219.

After the end of the Punic war, Carthage fell into trouble with her hired soldiers, and did not interfere with the Romans for a long time, while they went on to arrange the government of Sicily into what they called a province, which was ruled by a proprætor for a year after his magistracy at home. The Greek kingdom of Syracuse indeed still remained as an ally of Rome, and Messina and a few other cities were allowed to choose their own magistrates and govern themselves.

Soon after, Sardinia and Corsica were given up to the Romans by the hired armies of the Carthaginians, and as the natives fought hard against Rome, when they were conquered they were for the most part sold as slaves. These two islands likewise had a proprætor.

The Romans now had all the peninsula south of themselves, and as far north as Ariminim (now shortened into Rimini), but all beyond belonged to the Gauls —the Cisalpine Gauls, or Gauls on this side the Alps, as the Romans called them; while those on the other side were called Transalpine Gauls, or Gauls across the Alps. These northern Gauls were gathering again for an inroad on the south, and in the midst of the rumors of this danger there was a great thunderstorm at Rome, and the Capitol was struck by lightning. The Sybilline books were searched into to see what this might mean, and a warning was found, "Beware of the Gauls." Moreover, there was a saying that the Greeks and Gauls should one day enjoy the Forum; but the Romans fancied they could satisfy this prophecy by burying a man and woman of each nation, slaves, in the middle of the Forum, and then they prepared to attack the Gauls in their own country before the inroad could be made. There was a great deal of hard fighting, lasting for years; and in the course of it the consul, Caius Flaminius, began the great road which has since been called after him the Flaminian Way, and was the great northern road from Rome, as the Appian Way was the southern.

gaul
THE WOUNDED GAUL.

The great hero of the war was Marcus Claudius Marcellus, who had already made himself known for his dauntless courage. As consul, he fought a desperate battle on the banks of the Po with the Gauls of both sides the Alps, and himself killed their king or chief, Viridomar. He brought the spoils to Rome, and hung them in the Temple of Jupiter. It was only the third time in the history of Rome that such a thing had been done. Cisalpine Gaul was thus subdued, and another road was made to secure it; while in the short peace that followed the gates of the Temple of Janus were shut, having stood open ever since the reign of Numa.

The Romans were beginning to make their worship the same with that of the Greeks. They sent offerings to Greek temples, said that their old gods were the same as those of the Greeks, only under different names, and sent an embassy to Epidaurus to ask for a statue of Esculapius, the god of medicine and son of Phoebus Apollo. The emblem of Esculapius was a serpent, and tame serpents were kept about his temple at Epidaurus. One of these glided into the Roman galley that had come for the statue, and it was treated with great respect by all the crew until they sailed up the Tiber, when it made its way out of the vessel and swam to the island which had been formed by the settling of the mud round the heap of corn that had been thrown into the river when Porsena wasted the country. This was supposed to mean that the god himself took possession of the place, and a splendid temple there rose in his honor.

Another imitation of the Greeks which came into fashion at this time had a sad effect on the Romans. The old funerals in Greek poems had ended by games and struggles between swordsmen. Two brothers of the Brutus family first showed off such a game at their father's funeral, and it became a regular custom, not only at funerals, but whenever there was need to entertain the people, to show off fights of swordsmen. The soldier captives from conquered nations were used in this way; and some persons kept schools of slaves, who were trained for these fights and called gladiators. The battle was a real one, with sharp weapons, for life or death; and when a man was struck down, he was allowed to live or sentenced to death according as the spectators turned down or turned up their thumbs. The Romans fancied that the sight trained them to be brave, and to despise death and wounds; but the truth was that it only made them hard-hearted, and taught them to despise other people's pain —a very different thing from despising their own.

Another thing that did great harm was the making it lawful for a man to put away a wife who had no children. This ended by making the Romans much less careful to have one good wife, and the Roman ladies became much less noble and excellent than they had been in the good old days.

hannibal
HANNIBAL'S VOW.

In the meantime, the Carthaginians, having lost the three islands, began to spread their settlements further in Spain, where their chief colony was New Carthage, or, as we call it, Carthagena. The mountains were full of gold mines, and the Iberians, the nation who held them, were brave and warlike, so that there was much fighting to train up fresh armies. Hamilcar, the chief general in command there, had four sons, whom he said were lion whelps being bred up against Rome. He took them with him to Spain, and at a great sacrifice for the success of his arms the youngest and most promising, Hannibal, a boy of nine years old, was made to lay his hand on the altar of Baal and take an oath that he would always be the enemy of the Romans. Hamilcar was killed in battle, but Hannibal grew up to be all that he had hoped, and at twenty-six was in command of the army. He threatened the Iberians of Saguntum, who sent to ask help from Rome. A message was sent to him to forbid him to disturb the ally of Rome; but he had made up his mind for war, and never even asked the Senate of Carthage what was to be done, but went on with the siege of Saguntum. Rome was busy with a war in Illyria, and could send no help, and the Saguntines held out with the greatest bravery and constancy, month after month, till they were all on the point of starvation, then kindled a great fire, slew all their wives and children, and let Hannibal win nothing but a pile of smoking ruins.

pyrnees
IN THE PYRENEES.

Again the Romans sent to Carthage to complain, but the Senate there had made up their minds that war there must be, and that it was a good time when Rome had a war in Illyria on her hands, and Cisalpine Gaul hardly subdued; and they had such a general as Hannibal, though they did not know what a wonderful scheme he had in his mind, namely, to make his way by land from Spain to Italy, gaining the help of the Gauls, and stirring up all those nations of Italy who had fought so long against Rome. His march, which marks the beginning of the Second Punic War, started from the banks of the Ebro in the beginning of the summer of 219. His army was 20,000 foot and 12,000 horse, partly Carthaginian, partly Gaul and Iberian. The horsemen were Moorish, and he had thirty-seven elephants. He left his brother Hasdrubal with 10,000 men at the foot of the Pyrenees and pushed on, but he could not reach the Alps before the late autumn, and his passage is one of the greatest wonders of history. Roads there were none, and he had to force his way up the passes of the Little St. Bernard through snow and ice, terrible to the men and animals of Africa, and fighting all the way, so that men and horses perished in great numbers, and only seven of the elephants were left when he at length descended into the plains of Northern Italy, where he hoped the Cisalpine Gauls would welcome him.

CHAPTER XIX.
THE SECOND PUNIC WAR.

219.

When the Romans heard that Hannibal had passed the Pyrenees, they had two armies on foot, one under Publius Cornelius Scipio, which was to go to Spain, and the other under Tiberius Sempronius Longus, to attack Africa. They changed their plan, and kept Sempronius to defend Italy, while Scipio went by sea to Marsala, a Greek colony in Gaul, to try to stop Hannibal at the Rhone; but he was too late, and therefore, sending on most of his army to Spain, he came back himself with his choicest troops. With these he tried to stop the enemy from crossing the river Ticinus, but he was defeated and so badly wounded that his life was only saved by the bravery of his son, who led him out of the battle.

hannibal
MEETING OF HANNIBAL AND SCIPIO AT ZAMA.

Before he was able to join the army again, Sempronius had fought another battle with Hannibal on the banks of the Trebia and suffered a terrible defeat. But winter now came on, and the Carthaginians found it very hard to bear in the marshes of the Arno. Hannibal himself was so ill that he only owed his life to the last of his elephants, which carried him safely through when he was almost blind, and in the end he lost an eye. In the spring he went on ravaging the country in hopes to make the two new consuls, Flaminius and Servilius, fight with him, but they were too cautious, until at last Flaminius attacked him in a heavy fog on the shore of Lake Trasimenus. It is said that an earthquake shook the ground, and that the eager warriors never perceived it; but again the Romans lost, Flaminius was killed, and there was a dreadful slaughter, for Hannibal had sworn to give no quarter to a Roman. The only thing that was hopeful for Rome was that neither Gauls, Etruscans, nor Italians showed any desire to rise in favor of Hannibal; and though he was now very near Rome, he durst not besiege it without the help of the people around to bring him supplies, so he only marched southwards, hoping to gain the support of the Greek colonies. A dictator was appointed, Quintus Fabius Maximus, who saw that, by strengthening all the garrisons in the towns and cutting off all provisions, he should wear the enemy out at last. As he always put off a battle, he was called Cunctator, or the Delayer; but at last he had the Carthaginians enclosed as in a trap in the valley of the river Vulturnus, and hoped to cut them off, posting men in ambush to fall on them on their morning's march. Hannibal guessed that this must be the plan; and at night he had the cattle in the camp collected, fastened torches to their horns, and drove them up the hills. The Romans, fancying themselves surrounded by the enemy, came out of their hiding-places to fall back on the camp, and Hannibal and his army safely escaped. This mischance made the Romans weary of the Delayer's policy, and when the year was out, and two consuls came in, though one of them, Lucius Æmilius Paulus, would have gone on in the same cautious plan of starving Hannibal out without a battle, the other, Caius Terentius Varro, who commanded on alternate days with him, was determined on a battle. Hannibal so contrived that it was fought on the plain of Cannæ, where there was plenty of space to use his Moorish horse. It was Varro's day of command, and he dashed at the centre of the enemy; Hannibal opened a space for him, then closed in on both sides with his terrible horse, and made a regular slaughter of the Romans. The last time that the consul Æmilius was seen was by a tribune named Lentulus, who found him sitting on a stone faint and bleeding, and would have given him his own horse to escape, but Æmilius answered that he had no mind to have to accuse his comrade of rashness, and had rather die. A troop of enemies coming up, Lentulus rode off, and looking back, saw his consul fall, pierced with darts. So many Romans had been killed, that Hannibal sent to Carthage a basket containing 10,000 of the gold rings worn by the knights.

archimedes
ARCHIMEDES.

Hannibal was only five days' march beyond Rome, and his officers wanted him to turn back and attack it in the first shock of the defeat, but he could not expect to succeed without more aid from home, and he wanted to win over the Greek cities of the south; so he wintered in Campania, waiting for the fresh troops he expected from Africa or from Spain, where his brother Mago was preparing an army. But the Carthaginians did not care about Hannibal's campaigns in Italy, and sent no help; and Publius Cornelius Scipio and his brother, with a Roman army in Spain, were watching Mago and preventing him from marching, until at last he gave them battle and defeated and killed them both. But he was not allowed to go to Italy to his brother, who, in the meantime, found his army so unstrung and ill-disciplined in the delightful but languid Campania, that the Romans declared the luxuries of Capua were their best allies. He stayed in the south, however, trying to gain the alliance of the king of Macedon, and stirring up Syracuse to revolt. Marcellus, who was consul for the third time, was sent to reduce the city, which made a famous defence, for it contained Archimedes, the greatest mathematician of his time, who devised wonderful machines for crushing the besiegers in unexpected ways; but at last Marcellus found a weak part of the walls and surprised the citizens. He had given orders that Archimedes should be saved, but a soldier broke into the philosopher's room without knowing him, and found him so intent on his study that he had never heard the storming of the city. The man brandished his sword. "Only wait," muttered Archimedes, "till I have found out my problem;" but the man, not understanding him, killed him.

Hannibal remained in Italy, maintaining himself there with wonderful skill, though with none of the hopes with which he had set out. His brother Hasdrubal did succeed in leaving Spain with an army to help him, but was met on the river Metaurus by Tiberius Claudius Nero, beaten, and slain. His head was cut off by Nero's order, and thrown into Hannibal's camp to give tidings of his fate.

Young Scipio, meantime, had been sent to Spain, where he gained great advantages, winning the friendship of the Iberians, and gaining town after town till Mago had little left but Gades and the extreme south. Scipio was one of the noblest of the Romans, brave, pious, and what was more unusual, of such sweet and winning temper, that it was said of him that wherever he went he might have been a king.

On returning to Rome, he showed the Senate that the best way to get Hannibal out of Italy was to attack Africa. Cautious old Fabius doubted, but Scipio was sent to Sicily, where he made an alliance with Massinissa, the Moorish king in Africa; and, obtaining leave to carry out his plan, he was sent thither, and so alarmed Carthage, that Hannibal was recalled to defend his own country, where he had not been since he was a child. A great battle took place at Zama between him and Hannibal, in which Scipio was the conqueror, and the loss of Carthage was so terrible that the Romans were ready to have marched in on her and made her their subject, but Scipio persuaded them to be forbearing. Carthage was to pay an immense tribute, and swear never to make war on any ally of Rome. And thus ended the Second Punic War, in the year 201.

CHAPTER XX.
THE FIRST EASTERN WAR.

215-183.

Scipio remained in Africa till he had arranged matters and won such a claim to Massinissa's gratitude that this king of Numidia was sure to watch over the interests of Rome. Scipio then returned home, and entered Rome with a grand triumph, all the nobler for himself that he did not lead Hannibal in his chains. He had been too generous to demand that so brave an enemy should be delivered up to him. He received the surname of Africanus, and was one of the most respected and beloved of Romans. He was the first who began to take up Greek learning and culture, and to exchange the old Roman ruggedness for the graces of philosophy and poetry. Indeed the Romans were beginning to have much to do with the Greeks, and the war they entered upon now was the first for the sake of spreading their own power. All the former ones had been in self-defence, and the new one did in fact spring out of the Punic war, for the Carthaginians had tried to persuade Philip, king of Macedon, to follow in the track of Pyrrhus, and come and help Hannibal in Southern Italy. The Romans had kept him off by stirring up the robber Ætolians against him; and when he began to punish these wild neighbors, the Romans leagued themselves with the old Greek cities which Macedon oppressed, and a great war took place.

Titus Quinctius Flaminius commanded in Greece for four years, first as consul and then as proconsul. His crowning victory was at Cynocephalæ, or the Dogshead Rocks, where he so broke the strength of Macedon that at the Isthmian games he proclaimed the deliverance of Greece, and in their joy the people crowded round him with crowns and garlands, and shouted so loud that birds in the air were said to have dropped down at the sound.

Macedon had cities in Asia Minor, and the king of Syria's enemy, Antiochus the Great, hoped to master them, and even to conquer Greece by the help of Hannibal, who had found himself unable to live in Carthage after his defeat, and was wandering about to give his services to any one who was a foe of Rome.

As Rome took the part of Philip, as her subject and ally, there was soon full scope for his efforts; but the Syrians were such wretched troops that even Hannibal could do nothing with them, and the king himself would not attend to his advice, but wasted his time in pleasure in the isle of Euboea. So the consul Acilius first beat them at Thermopylæ, and then, on Lucius Cornelius Scipio being sent to conduct the war, his great brother Africanus volunteered to go with him as his lieutenant, and together they followed Antiochus into Asia Minor, and gained such advantages that the Syrian was obliged to sue for peace. The Romans replied by requiring of him to give up all Asia Minor as far as Mount Tarsus, and in despair he risked a battle in Magnesia, and met with a total defeat; 80,000 Greeks and Syrians being overthrown by 50,000 Romans. Neither Africanus nor Hannibal were present in this battle, since the first was ill, and the second was besieged in a city in Pamphylia; but while terms of peace were being made, the two are said have met on friendly terms, and Scipio asked Hannibal whom he thought the greatest of generals. "Alexander," was the answer. "Whom the next greatest?" "Pyrrhus." "Whom do you rank as the third?" "Myself," said Hannibal. "But if you had beaten me?" asked Scipio. "Then I would have placed myself before Alexander."

hannibal
HANNIBAL

The Romans insisted that Hannibal should be dismissed by Antiochus, though Scipio declared that this was ungenerous; but they dreaded his never-ceasing enmity; and when he took refuge with the king of Bothnia, they still required that he should be given up or driven a way. On this, Hannibal, worn-out and disappointed, put an end to his own life by poison, saying he would rid the Romans of their fear of an old man.

The provinces taken from Antiochus were given to Eumenes, king of Pergamus, who was to reign over them as tributary to the Romans. Lucius Scipio received the surname of Asiaticus, and the two brothers returned to Rome; but they had been too generous and merciful to the conquered to suit the grasping spirit that had begun to prevail at Rome, and directly after his triumph Lucius was accused of having taken to himself an undue share of the spoil. His brother was too indignant at the shameful accusation to think of letting him justify himself, but tore up his accounts in the face of the people. The tribune, Nævius, thereupon spitefully called upon him to give an account of the spoil of Carthage taken twenty years before. The only reply he gave was to exclaim, "This is the day of the victory of Zama. Let us give thanks to the gods for it;" and he led all that was noble and good in Rome with him to the temple of Jupiter and offered the anniversary sacrifice. No one durst say another word against him or his brother; but he did not choose to remain among the citizens who had thus insulted him, but went away to his estate at Liternum, and when he died, desired to be buried there, saying that he would not even leave his bones to his ungrateful country. The Cornelian family was the only one among the higher Romans who buried instead of burning their dead. He left no son, only a daughter, who was married to Tiberius Sempronius Gracchus, a brave officer who was among those who were sent to finish reducing Spain. It was a long, terrible war, fought city by city, inch by inch; but Gracchus is said to have taken no less than three hundred fortresses. But he was a milder conqueror than some of the Romans, and tried to tame and civilize the wild races instead of treating them with the terrible severity shown by Marcus Porcius Cato, the sternest of all old Romans. However, by the year 178 Spain had been reduced to obedience, and the cities and the coast were in good order, though the mountains harbored fierce tribes always ready for revolt.

Gracchus died early, and Cornelia, his widow, devoted herself to the cause of his three children, refusing to be married again, which was very uncommon in a Roman lady. When a lady asked her to show her her ornaments, she called her two boys, Tiberius and Caius, and their sister Sempronia, and said, "These are my jewels;" and when she was complimented on being the daughter of Africanus, she said that the honor she should care more for was the being called "the mother of the Gracchi."

It was not, however, one of her sons that was chosen to carry on their grandfather's name and the sacrifices of the Cornelian family. Probably Caius was not born when Scipio died, for his choice had been the second son of his sister and of Lucius Æmilius Paulus (son of him who died at Cannæ.) This child being adopted by his uncle, was called Publius Cornelius Scipio Æmilianus, and when he grew up was to marry his cousin Sempronia.